INDIAN SOCIETY AND POLITY

INDIAN SOCIETY AND POLITY

Joseph Benjamin

GYAN

ISBN : 978-81-212-1307-3

Price : ₹ 590

First Published, 2015

Published by

Gyan Publishing House
5, Ansari Road
Daryaganj, New Delhi-110002
Phones: 9811692060
E-mail: books@gyanbooks.com

Printed at: G. Print Process, Delhi.

Cataloging in Publication Data—DK
Courtesy: D.K. Agencies (P) Ltd. <docinfo@dkagencies.com>

Benjamin, Joseph, 1959- author.
Indian society and polity / Joseph Benjamin.
pages cm
Includes bibliographical references and index.
ISBN 9788121213073

1. People with social disabilities—Government policy—India. 2. People with social disabilities—Education (Higher)—India. 3. Poverty—Government policy—India. 4. Constitutional law—India. 5. Political questions and judicial power—India. 6. Social justice—India. I. Title.

HV1559.I4B46 2015 DDC 305.5680954 23

Contents

Preface

Indian society is full of problems, though effort is being taken to ameliorate such problems with the help of government and non-governmental organisations. In this present book effort is being made to study the major issues that have been present in our Indian society and polity since long. After independence, the framers of Indian Constitution have taken initiative to find solution of problem by incorporating certain provisions in the constitution. The ancient and medieval Indian society was full of caste discrimination. The framers of constitution have incorporated various provisions for dalits in making them at par with others. Indian constitution is a catalyst for social justice for weaker section of our Indian society.

Higher education for marginalised group was considered to be a nightmare. After independence for many years, weaker sections were not able to go for higher education. The enrollment for weaker section was abysmal. Right to Education Act 2009 has become a ray of hope for marginalised groups for education. Now education has become fundamental right for all Indian. All Indian, especially weaker section must get a seat in educational institution aided by government. It should be mandatory for the children of below 14 years to be present in the school. Mid-day meal will serve as a catalyst for the economically backward students (children) for enrollment. Literary drive is the sole motto of government.

Reservation in employment, education and political field has been in existence since independence. Initially, the reservation policy was for ten years. It is being extended every time for another ten years. Today it has become an electoral ploy for political parties. It is gradually extended to Other Backward Classes (OBCs), Muslim and Maratha. Is this a means for marginalised class for upward mobility or ways to get votes from weaker sections? How long the reservation policy has to go?

There has been number of UN conventions and constitutional provisions in India for the protection of children from exploitation. Still one finds that the status of children has not been improved. There are so many children working in hazardous factories. Poverty compels these children to work in factories and canteens. After independence, Indian government undertook massive efforts to eradicate poverty from India. There is a very close link between poverty and malnutrition in India. It is poverty that leads to malnutrition and malnutrition leads to diseases, ill-health and ultimately the result is death. In order to overcome with the problem of malnutrition the first step that government has to take is to remove poverty. Poverty is the major cause of malnutrition.

Globalisation is the process of social transformation. Globalisation has helped in socio-economic progress of developing countries in general and India in particular. Globalisation is understood as rapid increase in cross-border economic, social and technological exchange. It is a process which leads to greater interdependence and mutual awareness among economic, political and social units in the world. The promoters of globalisation always try to convince the world that it will create a new economic and social order. Around 70 per cent Indian consumer live in the rural areas. They are mostly illiterate and exploited brazenly. They are exploited in the rural market on account of lack of competition among sellers since there are only one or two petty shops available in rural places and the consumers have no choice. Today, Judicial Activism has come as a saviour for all, executive, legislature and especially for poor masses. There is no doubt that judicial activism is to be considered as a vanguard of Indian democracy.

In preparing this book, I have been supported by my family members; my wife Smt. Pratibha, my sons namely, Prashant and Jayant who have shown patience during my work.

I will be happy to have comments and feedback on this book entitled, ***Indian Society and Polity.***

Joseph Benjamin

1

Indian Constitution: A Catalyst for Social Justice

Social Justice is the only means to unite Indians together and to transform the subcontinent into an egalitarian truly welfare state. And that's why the founding fathers of our Constitution stressed the paramount need of social justice in various fields of people's life. The concept of Social Justice is present in our Indian Constitution but the need is to give it a practical shape in its various dimensions. It can be made more effective, if we keep it above the politics of vote banks, immoral elections, hinged on money, muscle power and corruption. The concept of Social Justice is essentially based on the philosophy of Humanism.

The ideology of Social Justice stands for the legitimate rights of the poor. Thinkers and social reformers like Dr. B.R. Ambedkar, Dr. Ram Manohar Lohia, and Mahatma Jotiba Phule treat Social Justice as a true basis of patriotism and nationalism. Dr. Ambedkar, a revolutionary leader, has devoted to the cause of the downtrodden of India. He is regarded as messiah of social justice as well as a strong foe of social slavery. Justice for Dr. Ambedkar is simply another name for liberty, equality and fraternity.[1] This forms the corner stone of Dr. Ambedkar's concept of social justice. It upholds the dignity of human personality. As a chief architect of Indian Constitution, he got it shaped clearly on the principles of justice, liberty, equality, fraternity and dignity of human beings. These principles of social justice denote brotherly relations of a citizen with every other citizen in our Indian society. The other precepts of social justice are the supremacy of Constitutional rule, equality before law and fundamental rights. According to Dr. Ambedkar, the concept of social justice is a problem not merely of distributing the material abundance among the people but basically a mode of life based on mutual respect and regard, a feeling of brotherhood and equal members of a society.

Definition

Justice for Plato, a Greek Philosopher, was supreme virtue, which defines goodness in human being. "Social justice may be defined as the principle of a society, consisting of different type of man .... who have combined under the impulse of their need of one another, and by their combination in one society, and their concentration on their separate functions, have made a whole which is perfect because it is the product and the image of the whole of the human mind."[2]

Another Greek Philosopher, Aristotle summed up political understanding about the nature of human beings when he says, "man, when perfected, is the best of the animals; but if he be isolated from "*Noma*" and "*Dike*" he is worst of all. In the view of the general conception of justice it may be rightly be explained that to Aristotle, the spirit of social justice lies in just arrangement of society which would mean a model in which each one does efficiently the work for which one is fitted by nature of one's capacities and abilities, and receives accordingly what is necessary to enable him to continue his work. Though the state regulations can only be accepted as general, not as applying to every individual instance, yet the laws of a state as Aristotle urged, can only provide for what is best in general. In Aristotle's idea of social justice, the supremacy of Law is accepted as a mark of a good state in comparison to the class of wise rulers.

John Rawls (1921-2002), an American modern philosopher, has developed the idea of Justice in his famous book, *A Theory of Justice* in 1971. John Rawls started working on the idea of justice as fairness in 1957 when he published his 9 pages article in the Journal of Philosophy. He was the first liberal thinker who gave importance to

Justice.[3] Rawls argues that this society is a well-ordered society, which is committed to the welfare of its members and is regulated by a public sense of justice. Rawls theory of justice is based on two principles, namely, (i) each person is to have an equal right to the most extensive basic liberty compatible with similar liberty for others. (ii) Social and economic inequalities are to be arranged so that they are both (a) reasonably expected to be to everyone's advantages, and (b) attached to positions and offices open to all.

Indian Philosophy and Social Justice

The theory of social justice in the Buddhist way of life is purely humanistic and secular. It did not find any reason for classifying human beings as it was done in *Manusmirti*. The Jain way of life, too, endeavoured to seek social harmony and justice through righteous conduct of the individual. Unless an individual was prepared to show respect for the lives of other individual, there could be no just order of human relation.

Various religions like Islam, Christianity, Judaism, Sikhism, Jainism, and Zoroastrianism have different views of social justice. Each one saw its concept as a manifestation of divine Law as revealed to their respective prophets/Gods. These religions contains a set of social rules in the light of which, a community, a social order, has to be established and maintained. In Christianity, the principle of social justice lies in the teaching, love God, and love man and practice righteous conduct. Virtuous conduct towards all is the basis of social justice. All human beings are children of God. God is the distributor of justice. Judaism regard social justice wholly dependent on God's will; Judaism still is the main source of their social order. Thus justice in various fields is influenced or dominated by religion; and social justice is nothing but to do certain permitted things and to negate those, which are not allowed to be done. The basic source of social justice is religion.

The saints of medieval India endeavoured to seek and strengthen the spirit of social justice through the grace of God. In medieval India social justice was linked with the kingdom of *Ishwar*, God or Allah; the situation, good or bad, was acclaimed as the result of divine justice; and it was also thought that ultimately after death justice would be done to all.

The social philosophy of *Varnashram Dharma*, resulting in caste and untouchability had broken the unity of Indian national life. It was Kabir who stood for drastic changes in the existing social order and values, which could restore to man his proper place in society. He challenged the divinity of *Varnashram Dharma* and doubted the authority of *Vedas, Upanishads, Epics, Smritis* and other sacred books.

Social Justice is that sort of justice which prescribes certain ideals closely related to human society; it sustains the existence and continuity of the individual, family, society and the nation; its implementation safeguards the interests of the weaker sections of society; and this removes all the serious unjust found between man and man, so that the lines of all the citizens become improved and emancipated. As a result, every man, according to his own potentiality and merit, may participate in the power and wealth of the nation and may avail social status of his own liking and outlook. Social Justice has been explained through various constitutional provisions. There are various constitutional provisions in Indian Constitution, which are supposed to provide Social Justice to all in general and weaker sections of society in particular.

Social Justice is multi-dimensional, its scope is very wide, and a large number of agencies are required to make it more effective. Social Justice is not a thing, which can be achieved in a stipulated period. Weaker sections of our society were exploited for centuries. It has been more than 60 years since the enforcement of Constitution, still many weaker section lags behind. In this Chapter an effort is made to study various constitutional provisions, which provides social justice to all and especially to weaker section. It would be an effort to review the governmental programmes, which provide social justice to weaker section of our society.

Indian Constitution and Social Justice:

The Indian Constitution has numerous provisions, which provides Social Justice; but no government would be wholly in a position to implement all its provisions in the interest of the weaker sections of society. The Preamble of the Constitution has tried to provide its citizens:

> *Justice, social, economic and political,*
>
> *Liberty of thought, expression, belief, faith and worship;*
>
> *Equality of status and of opportunity, and to promote among them all*
>
> *Fraternity assuring the dignity of the individual and the unity and integrity of the Nation.*

The Preamble itself says that our constitution is based on the socialistic principles.[4] Constitution of India gives some important provisions which guarantees social justice to Scheduled Castes/ Tribes/Women/Backward Classes. The Fundamental Rights of Indian Constitution from Article 12 to 35 speaks of basic right of its citizens. Article14 enunciates the right to equality. Scheduled Castes have been for centuries discriminated against and denied equality and human dignity by the rest of society. It says,

> *The State shall not deny to any person equality before the law or the equal protection of the laws within the territory of India.*

Louis Dumont in his book *Homo Hierarchicus* (1970) has described India as a country where a hierarchical value system prevails, which regards human being as belonging to high and low. We have in our Indian society highborn, lowborn and the last born. Article 14 guarantees the right to equality and human dignity of all citizens. Article 15 prohibits discrimination on grounds of religions, race, caste, sex or place of birth and Article 25 guarantees the right to freedom of conscience and freedom to profess and practice religion.

Clause 4 of Art.15 makes special provisions for the State to take up programmers for the advancement of socially and educationally backward class and for Scheduled Castes and Scheduled Tribes. This provision was necessitated by the court decision in the *State of Madras vs. Champakam* in 1951. Article 15 (4) says,

> *Nothing in this article or in clause (2) of article 29 shall prevent the state from making any special provision for the advancement of any socially and educationally backward classes of citizens or for the Scheduled Castes and Scheduled Tribes.*

Dr. Ambedkar did suggest that reservation of more than 50 per cent would seem to be unreasonable. But the Supreme Court has ruled no citizen of India can claim reservation either in jobs or in admission to educational institutions as a matter of right and reservation cannot be given at the cost of efficiency in administration and governance as per Article 335 of the constitution. Justice Cyriac Joseph and Justice S.B. Sinha said that reservation is a concession given to disadvantaged class of people as per Articles 15 and 16 of the Constitution but the concession cannot be given in the line with Article 335 of the Constitution which lays down that efficiency in administration and governance can not be lost sight of.[5]

Article 16 states, that there shall be equality of opportunity for all citizens in the matters relating employment or appointment to any office under the state. Article 16 (4) authorises the state to make special provisions for reservation posts in favour of any Backward Classes of citizen who are not adequately represented in the service of State. It says:

> *"Nothing in this Article shall prevent the State from making any provision for reservation of appointments or posts in favour of any backward class of citizen which, in the option of the State, is not adequately represented in the service under the State."*

Again Article 16 (4A) reads,[6]

> *Nothing in this article shall prevent the State from making any provision for reservation*[7] *(in matters of promotion, with consequent seniority, to any class) or classes of posts in services under the State in favour of Scheduled Castes and Scheduled Tribes, which in opinion of the State are not adequately represented in the service under the State.*

Similarly Article 16 (4 B)[8] says:

> *Nothing in this Article shall prevent the State from considering any unfilled vacancies of a year which are reserved for being filled up in that year in accordance with any provision for reservation made under clause (4) or clause (4 A) as a separate class of vacancies to be filled up in any succeeding year or years and such class of vacancies shall not be considered together with the vacancies of the year in which they are being filled up for determining the ceiling of fifty per cent reservation on total number of vacancies of that year.*

But it has been noticed that after many years of effort for employment of scheduled Cates and Scheduled Tribes only 11.9 per cent are in-group A job, 13.7 per cent are in Group B, 16.4 per cent in Group C and 18. 3 per cent in group D in Central Government services (excluding sweeper).

Table 1: The representation of Scheduled Castes and Scheduled Tribes and OBCs in Central Government Services as on 1st January 2005

Group	Total	SCs	%	STs	%	OBCs	%
A	80,589	9,551	11.9	3,448	4.3	3,791	4.7
B	1, 39,958	19,194	13.7	6,230	4.5	3,252	2.3
C	20,36,103	3,33,708	16.4	1,31,678	6.5	1,19,968	5.9
D	7, 67,224	1,40,469	18.3	55,032	6.9	32,973	4.3

Source: India 2009 (Government of India Publication), p. 987.

Table 2: Reservation in all Categories (in 2011)

	SCs	*STs*		*STs*		*Top Level*	
Group A	11.1	4.6		Secretary	Ad. Secy	Jt. Secy	Director
Group B	14.3	5.5					
Group C	16.0	7.8	Total Officers	149	108	477	590
Group D*	19.3	7.0	SCs %	– (0%)	2(1.9%)	31(6.5%)	17. (2.9%)
Safai Karamchari	39.9	6.2	STs (%)	4(2.7%)	2(1.9%)	15(3.1%)	7(1.2%)

	SCs	***STs***		***STs***		***Top Level***	
Group A	11.1	4.6		***Secretary***	***Ad. Secy***	***Jt. Secy***	***Director***
Group B	14.3	5.5					
Group C	16.0	7.8	***Total Officers***	149	108	477	590
Group D*	19.3	7.0	SCs %	– (0%)	2(1.9%)	31(6.5%)	17. (2.9%)
Safai Karamchari	39.9	6.2	STs (%)	4(2.7%)	2(1.9%)	15(3.1%)	7(1.2%)
Total	**17.0**	**7.4**					

*Excluding Safai Karamchari

As on 1.1.2011

Source: *The Economic Times*, September 6, 2012.

There is not much improvement with regard to employment of weaker section in Group A, B, C and D. The table 1 and 2 gives the same percentage of employment of weaker section in all four groups. The government record *INDIA 2009* and *The Economic Times* provides the same figure. It will take long time to get their share in all categories of employment. There is slight improvement in category B, C and D. There is large number of weaker section in *Safai Karamchari.*

Reservation in Post and Service Bill: The reservation to Scheduled Castes and Scheduled Tribes and debate over it has come to fore with introduction and subsequent passing of Scheduled Castes and Scheduled Tribes (Reservation in Post and Service) Bill 2008 (Bill No. LXXIV) in *Rajya Sabha.*

The present Bill was introduced on December 12, 2008 which bars reservation to Scheduled Castes and Scheduled Tribes in temporary posts and in scientific and technical posts in 47 Central Universities and Institutions on the euphemism of institutes of excellence with the fear that reservation may reduce the efficiency and may hamper merit in these elite institutions. Article 4 (1) of the Bill prohibits reservation to Scheduled Castes and Scheduled Tribes in Central Universities that comprise 47 institutions. (See, *Hitavada,* (Nagpur daily) 22/2/2009)

Table 3: Representation of SCs in Teaching/Non-teaching Posts In Central Universities as on 1/1/1993

Position	*Total Employees*	*SC Employees*	*per cent SC Employees*
Professor	1,155	2	0.17
Reader/Associate Professor	1, 774	6	0.34
Lecturer/Assistant Proféssor/Director of Physical Education	1, 491	35	2.35
Research Associate/Tutor/Demonstrator	257	3	1.17
Group A, Non-Teaching	756	26	3.44
Group B, Non-Teaching	1, 525	49	3.21
Group C, Non-Teaching	9, 001	414	4.60
Group D, Non-Teaching	10, 635	2,368	22.27

Source: *Hitavada*, (Nagpur daily) 22/2/2009

Abolition of untouchability: Article.17 abolishes the inhuman practice of untouchability. Article says,

> *"Untouchability has been abolished and its practice in any form is forbidden. The enforcement of any disability arising out of Untouchability shall be an offence punishable in accordance with law.*

The Parliament in exercise of the powers conferred by Article 35 (ii) has enacted the Untouchability (Offence) Act, 1955. The basic objective of this enactment was to ban the practice of untouchability in any form. This Act of 1955 was again amended by the Parliament in 1976 by the Untouchability (Offence) Amendment Act, in order to make the law more stringent for removing untouchability from society in any case. This act was renamed as the Protection of Civil Act, 1955. Under the amended Act, any discrimination on the ground of untouchability is considered as an offence. The supreme Court in PUDR vs Union of India held that the fundamental rights under Article 17 of the Constitution is available against private individuals also and it is constitutional duty of the state to take necessary steps and ensure that this fundamental rights is not violated.[9] Articles 19, 23, 25, 29 and 30 guarantee protection from various forms of discrimination and spell out some basic rights of the people. These

Articles have special significance for the Scheduled Castes since they pertain to areas in which the Scheduled Castes are often discriminated against and their basic rights denied.

Article 19 says all citizens are allowed to form an association. And at same time it also allows practice of any profession, or to carry on any occupation, trade or business. But still in villages, the Scheduled Castes are not able to start new business. In the rural areas people still feel that scheduled castes should carry on their tradition occupation. Again the same Article guarantees Freedom of movement in any part of India. But it seems that Freedom of Movement is not application to Scheduled Castes and Scheduled Tribes. If *Tharu* tribes move from one place to another, he would be denied reservation Example *Tharu* in Bihar is not considered as Scheduled Tribes where as the same tribe in Uttar Predash is considered as Scheduled Tribes.

Article 23 prohibits traffic in human being and beggar and forced labourers. Article 23 (1) says that Traffic in human beings and beggar and other similar forms of forced labour are prohibited and any contravention of this provision shall be an offence punishable in accordance with law. Section 2 says,

> *"Nothing in this article shall prevent the state from imposing compulsory service for public purposes, and in imposing such service the State shall not make any discrimination on grounds only of religion, race, caste or any of them."*

But out of all Bonded Labourers most of them are Scheduled Castes. According to the National Commission for Scheduled Caste (SC) and Scheduled Tribes (ST), there are an estimated 115 millions children working in slavery, and amongst those, approximately 80-90 per cent are Dalits who work as bonded labour in order to pay off debt. (*National Commission for Scheduled Caste and Scheduled Tribes 2000)*

Article 24 prohibits employment of children in factories. It says,

> *"No child below the age of fourteen years shall be employed to work in any factory or mine or engaged in any other hazardous employment."*

Article 25 provides Right to Freedom of Religion to its citizens. But Scheduled Castes and Scheduled Tribes cannot embrace Religion other than Hinduism, Buddhism and Sikhism. If they embrace other religion they may not get concession provided to Scheduled Castes and Scheduled Tribes.

Soosai filed a writ petition (9596 of 1983) in Madras in 1983. He belonged to the *Adi dravida* community and was a convert to Christianity. He was a cobbler by caste in Chennai. In July 1982 the Regional Deputy Director of the Khadi and village Industries Board allotted several cobblers bunks free of cost. But Soosai was not. On the inquiry, the petitioner came to know that the allotment of bunks, free of cost, was a special Central Assistance Scheme for the welfare of the Scheduled Castes and that the Order of the Social Welfare Department granting this programme had specification stated that persons belonging to Scheduled Castes converted to Christianity were not eligible for assistance under the scheme.[10] Again second writ petition (1017 of 1984) was filed seeking relief of Government circular of Government of Tamil Nadu to Tamil Nadu Public Service Commission stating that Scheduled castes converts to Christianity who revert to Hinduism and on that basis obtain appointment to reserved seats in Government services, and having done so change their religion once again after their entry into government services, are eligible to have their selection cancelled. The Order violates the fundamental rights of the Scheduled Castes to profess a religion of their choice. The petition was dismissed but the causal way the judgment has been written. The very serious question arises whether after conversion to Christianity caste still remains.

Article 29 of Indian Constitution provides protection to interests of Minorities. It says (1) any section of the citizens residing in the territory of India or any part thereof having a distinct language, script or culture of its own shall have the right to conserve the same. Again section 2 speaks,

> *"No citizen shall be denied admission into any educational institution maintained by the State or funds on grounds only of religion, race, caste, language or any of them."*

The history of this country from the time of Independence shows that certain minority communities have been able to preserve their culture and traditions and demand their rights in the matter of admission to educational institutions maintained by the State on the strength of this article. The judiciary has played a very important role in protecting the interests of minorities like the Muslims and the Christians particularly in respect of the establishment and management of their educational institutions. In the Gujarat University Case (1974) the Supreme Court ruled that the State could not interfere in the management of an institution established and run by a minority community.[11] The Janata Government set up in 1977 the Minorities Commission for the protecting the rights of the minorities.

Another very important article i.e., Article 38 says,

> *"The State shall strive promote the welfare of the people by securing and protecting as effectively as it may a social order in which justice, social, economic and political shall inform all the institutions of the national life."*[12]

Clause 2 says that the State to ensure the creation of a social order with justice and to strive to minimize inequalities in income, status and opportunities and to bring about an equitable distribution of resources.

Article 46 directs the State to promote the educational and economic interests of weaker sections especially, those of Scheduled Castes and /Scheduled Tribes. Article 164 also provides for the appointment of a special minister in certain cases. Article 164 (1) states that,

> *"The Chief Minister shall be appointed by the Governor and the other Ministers shall be appointed by Governor on the advice of the Chief Minister, and the Minister shall hold office during the pleasure of the Governor."*

Provided that in the state of Bihar, Madhya Pradesh and Orissa, there shall be a Minister in charge of tribal welfare who may in addition be in charge of the welfare of the Scheduled Castes and backward classes or any other work. So the Constitution speaks of the welfare of weaker section of society. In these following states there is provision for Minister for Scheduled Castes and Scheduled Tribes who will look after the interests of these weaker sections in the state.

Articles 330 and 332 provide for reservation of seats for the Scheduled Castes and Scheduled Tribes in Lok-Sabha and the Vidhan-Sabha respectively. A fixed per cent of members of Lok Sabha and of the Vidhan Sabha belong to Scheduled Casts and Scheduled tribes. Till 14th Lok Sabha election the reservation of seat for Scheduled Castes and Scheduled Tribes were 79 and 41 respectively. Today during 15th general election, the seats are distributed as per their population in India. Today the reservation of seats for Scheduled Cates and Scheduled Tribes are 84 and 47 respectively as per Representation of People Act 1950 in 2008 vide Representation of People Act 2008.[13]

Article335 requires that the claims of the members of the Scheduled Castes be taken into account while making appointment to services. This article speaks,

> *"The claims of the members of the scheduled castes and the scheduled tribes shall be taken into consideration, consistently with the maintenance of efficiency of administration, in the making of appointments to services and posts in connection with the affairs of the Union or of a State.*

Article 338 provides for appointment by President of a special officer for the Scheduled Castes and Scheduled Tribes in order to investigate matters relating to the safeguards provided for them under the Constitution. The Commission will be known as the National Commission for the Scheduled Castes and Scheduled Tribes. The Commissioner of Scheduled Castes and Scheduled Tribes has to submit report to the President of India, which is also presented to the parliament. There is a special wing also in the Home of Ministry, which deals with problem of Scheduled Castes.[14]

Article 341 empowers the Presidents to identify the Castes/ Races/Tribes or parts of or groups within them to be Scheduled Caste communities. Article 341 (2) states that,

> *"Parliament may by law include in or exclude from the list of scheduled castes specified in a notification issued under clause (1) any caste, race or tribe or part of or group within any caste, race or tribe, but save as aforesaid a notification issued under the said clause shall not be varied by any subsequent notification."*

There are numerous provisions mentioned in the Indian Constitution for upliftment of Scheduled Castes, Scheduled Tribes and Other Backward Classes. It seems it will take a long way to achieve the goal of development for the *dalits*.

Conclusion

All these provisions provided in the Constitution guarantee the development and welfare of *dalit* in India. The Government has introduced National Rural Employment Guarantee Act. This scheme provides at least 100 days employment for rural people. The National Commission of Enterprises in the Unorganised Sectors (NCEUS) in its report said that "in district where more than 50 per cent of the working population belong to Scheduled Castes and Scheduled Tribes the cap of 100 days of employment should be removed".[15] If one reviews the development of *dalit* it is found that there is still lot to be done. In urban cities there is a snail like progress but in rural area it needs the attention of government. The National Commission of Enterprises in the Unorganised Sectors (NCEUS) has analysed the development of the ten years from 1993-94 to 2004-05. The Commission has found impressive rate of growth of Gross Domestic Product (GDP) but the benefits of growth bypassed the over-whelming majority of India's population. Although the people suffering from extreme poverty and living below the so-called officially poverty line (of a per capita consumption of Rs 27 per day in 2012-13) came down during this period, they seemed to have moved up only marginally. The data shows that only 23 per cent of the population- the middle class and the higher income groups captured most of the benefits of high-income growth. The remaining 77 per cent were stuck below the average consumption of Rs 20 per day. These poor and vulnerable groups comprised 88 per cent of our SCs/

STs population, 80 per cent of OBCs, and 85 per cent of the Muslims.[16] Most of these are illiterate and without even primary education. These groups appear to be a combination of the socially discriminated and educationally deprived and economic destitute. Constitution is the only means through which social justice can be provided as it has legal sanction behind it. During last sixty years of our independence the march towards social egalitarianism has known no obstacles, which has not been overcome. In the same breath it has to be conceded that it is a long haul.

Endnotes

1. Dr. Babasaheb Ambedkar *Writings and speeches,* Vol. 3, 1987, p. 25.
2. C.L. Wayper: Political Thought, 1958, p. 29.
3. John Rawls, A Theory of Justice, 1971.
4. The word socialist was added in Preamble according to 42nd Amendment Act, 1976.
5. They delivered judgment on the appeal of Andhra Pradesh Public Service Commission against the judgment of the A P High Court dated july 23, 2008 holding that reservation to Scheduled Castes, Scheduled Tribes and Other Backward Classes should be provided from the preliminary stage during recruitment in state services in group one and two categories. See *Hitavada*, April 21, 2009.
6. By 77th amendment Act 1995, sec. 2.
7. By 85th Amendment Act 2001.
8. By 81st Amendment Act 2000, sec. 2 w.e.f. 9/6/2000.
9. AIR 1982, SC 1473.
10. The Presidential Order, 1950 states that no person who professes a religion different from the Hindu or the Sikh religion shall be deemed to be a member of a Scheduled Castes. The Presidential Order of 1950 was amended in 1956 and 1990. Dalit belonging to Hinduism, Sikhism and Buddhism were given special privilege on the ground that dalit are socially, politically, economically and educationally weak. For Detail See Jose Kananaikal, "Scheduled Castes Converts in Search of Justice: In the Hall of Supreme

Court," *Social Action*, Vol. 36, No. 1, Jan-March, 1985, pp. 101-107.

11. St. Xaviers' College Society of Ahmedabad vs. State of Gujarat, 1974 I SCC 717.
12. Article 38 renumbered as clause (1) thereof by the 44th Constitutional Act 1978, Sec. 9.
13. See Representation of People Amendment Act 2008.
14. Also see, 89th Amendment Act 2003.
15. Panel for removal of 100-days cap in job guarantee scheme, *Hitavada*, May 7, 2009, p. 8.
16. Arjun Sengupta, "Unfinished Agenda" *Deccan Chronicle (Hydrabad)* , May 4, 2009,.

2

Higher Education for Marginalised Groups in India: An Evaluation

Introduction

For years together government of India has been trying its level best to uplift the weaker section of society. The main objective of Indian Education system had been to provide education equal access to all. Affirmative action in the form of reservation has been accorded to Scheduled Castes/Scheduled Tribe and the other Backward Classes irrespective of gender divide. More than six decades of implementation of reservation in the field of education and more than 50 years of establishment of University Grants Commissions, still the weaker sections in India have not satisfactory access of higher education. They still lag behind in the field of elementary and higher education. No doubt we need to improve the quality in higher education but at same time we need to improve the lot of disadvantaged groups of Indian society. Many educational commissions had been set-up by Central government, yet not sufficient dent has been made on this intractable problem. The government spending on higher education has been increased to 6 per cent of the GDP from 3.8 per cent.

This chapter would evaluate the present Higher Education system and find out how this higher education is accessible to Scheduled Castes, Scheduled Tribes and OBCs. These communities still lag behind in the field of higher education even after sixty seven years of independence. In this chapter an effort is made to evaluate the level of education amongst Scheduled Castes, Scheduled Tribes and OBCs as they are considered to be fractured communities of Indian society.

Understanding Weaker Sections

Different scholars/social reformers have explained the concept of weaker sections in different ways. What we call *dalit*, weaker sections has been defined in variety of sub-names. They were called untouchables, *Harijans*, depressed classes, Scheduled Castes. The untouchables were characterised by the upper caste, social reformers, particularly in Maharashtra, in a variety of ways. For example, S. M. Mate, a Brahmin Social reformer in the 19th century Maharashtra, used the term *asprustha* for *dalits*, meaning the untouched rather than the untouchable.[1] Hindu society insists on the segregation of untouchables and does not allow them to live inside their main residential areas. They were generally required to live at a distance from the main village. Residential segregation was somewhat strictly enforced. Prabhu[2] mentions that untouchability refers to denying even human status to a group of human beings; this group is not even allowed the consideration, which may be shown to creatures like animals. Hanumantha Rao[3] says that untouchability is a feeling of pollution, defilement of contamination entertained by the non-scheduled castes towards scheduled castes and is caused by (a) touch, (b) sight, and (c) or by mere physical proximity of the scheduled castes persons. This pollution concept is institutionalised in the Hindu society through caste system. The stigma of untouchability is much more among Scheduled Castes than the Scheduled Tribes. The Scheduled tribes have certain culture that they carry on.

V.R. Shinde,[4] the Maratha social reformer, used depressed classes for *dalits* and thus located the term *dalit* in the imperial setting. Gradually this term was mentioned in the Census Report, 1921, but the castes constituting the depressed classes were not defined. Again, term the depressed class was used before 1930, but since the enactment of Government of India Act, 1935, they are consistently referred to as 'Scheduled Castes'. Later in Presidential Order of 1950 term the scheduled caste was entered in the Constitution for special treatment. The 'Scheduled Caste' means such castes, races, or tribes, or part of all groups within such castes, race or tribes, "as are deemed under Article 341 to be Scheduled Castes for the purposes of the Constitution." It was confined to only Hindu religion. Now after the amendment in the Presidential Order of 1950, it includes lower castes from Sikh, Buddhist religions. Now the Ranganath Mishra Committee has recommended in its report that *dalit* Christians may be included in the scheduled castes list for constitutional benefits. This is only a matter of time; they will be included in the scheduled.

Many others have also taken effort in naming weaker sections. Mahatma Gandhi introduced them *harijan,* which means 'children of god'. Many did not like the new name *harijan* and most of them have rejected the term. Though there were many discussions on the question of separate electorate for the *dalit* between Ambedkar and Gandhi. The category of *harijan* cannot be encapsulated within the *dalit* category since it is entirely 'metaphysical.' At the same time the term *harijan* is an ascribed one since it does not flow from the untouchables own experiences. Gandhi and those upper caste people who could not genuinely integrate them within their social consciousness despite its divine association artificially imposed it on the untouchables. The term *harijan* refers to an aggregate of many castes (which differ from each other) which had been reduced to the lowest ritual and social status under the caste hierarchy. Many feel that the word *harijan* has been wrongly translated as 'children of god' and some people do not like this concept.

Isaacs regards it, as a term of abuse meaning a person whose father is unknown,[5] as such the scheduled caste people have been handed over to '*Hari*' (god). So '*Hari*' (god) is only their father. Today the term *harijan* is not in use. As Dhananjay Keer [6] said that Dr. Ambedkar's followers resented the term '*harijan*' on being challenged to suggest a better term failed to do so. Overall, the term *harijan* lacks discursive. In the opinion of Gail Omvedt, 'the term *dalit* provides a militant alternative to the Gandhian term *harijan.*

Ambedkar himself first used the concept of *dalit* in his fortnightly magazine *Bahishkruit Bharat.* He defined it comprehensively: '*Dalithood*' is a kind of life condition, which characterises the exploitation, suppression and marginalisation of *dalits* by the social, economic, cultural and political domination of upper caste *Brahminical* order.[7] Even today many commonly use concept *dalit.* Ambedkar used this differently in different situation. While dealing with the imperial state he used the category of 'depressed classes'.[8] When he addressed the higher caste he used the category *bahishkruit* meaning totally outcaste.[9]

In more recent years the category *dalit* was first comprehensively deployed by the Panthar, thereby combining the caste, class and gender dimensions which were also part of Ambedkar's mode of thinking and his revolutionary politics.[10] The category *dalit* needs to be distinguishing from the terms backward and forward. It does not entertain such binary opposition because such binaries assume backwardness as a given in order to legitimise its distinction from forward.[11] This distinction may be like privilege and under privilege, which aimed at transcending all the constructs that underlie and renew the structures of inequality and exploitation. The same thing is also found in OBCs i.e., the OBCs of under privilege and creamy layer. The category *dalit* is also distanced from state constituted categories like Schedule Caste, Schedule Tribe and OBCs. These terms are entered in the constitution for the benefits to them. These terms may be considered as legal term constructed by the state.

To sum up the category of *dalit* means the class suppressed by the upper castes many years ago. They may fall in Hinduism, Sikhism and Buddhism. Today Christians also feel that castes exist in their religion. There is a higher caste Christian and lower caste Christian. Untouchability still prevails in Christianity basically in Southern India. The present chapter would study the educational level of Scheduled Castes and Scheduled Tribes.

Higher Education and Constitutional Provisions for SCs and STs

Higher Education in India is accessible to students from all social and economic background. As Article 15 (4) of Indian Constitution states that,

> *'Nothing in this Article or in clause (2) of Article 29 shall prevent the State from making any special provision for the advancement of any socially and educationally backward classes of citizens or for the Scheduled Castes and the scheduled tribes.*

The spread of education among the weaker sections has been a major part of the government programmes since the early 1950s. It mainly includes financial support in the forms of scholarship, stipends at the school and college levels, construction of hostels, reservations for students of this community in engineering and medical colleges and other facilities for Scheduled Castes, Scheduled Tribes and minorities. Article 46 of the Constitution of India refers to the special care to be taken by the state for the promotion of education among the scheduled castes and scheduled tribes. It states,

> *"The State shall promote, with special care, the education and economic interests of the weaker sections of people, and, in particular of the Scheduled Castes and Scheduled Tribes, and shall protect them from social injustice and all forms of social exploitation."*

Articles 330, 332, 335, 338 to 342 and the entire Fifth and Sixth Schedules of the Constitution deal with special provisions for implementation of the objectives set forth in Article 46. These provisions need to be fully utilised for the benefit of these weaker sections in our society.

After independence, the Government of India has taken a number of steps to strengthen the education base of persons belonging to the scheduled castes and scheduled tribes. At the University and Higher Education, the University Grants Commission (UGC) issued guidelines/directives/instructions from time to time for the implementation of reservation policy. The UGC implements the career orientation courses for Scheduled Castes, Scheduled Tribes and Minorities for entry in services. It recommends their candidature for teaching positions in universities and colleges. The UGC has introduced the scheme of establishment of Scheduled Castes/ Scheduled Tribes cells in universities in the year 1983. The UGC has also introduced various schemes for the benefit of the students of Scheduled Castes/Scheduled Tribes communities like coaching classes for Scheduled Castes/Scheduled Tribes candidates for preparation for National Eligibility Test (NET), residential coaching at UG/ PG level for Scheduled Castes/Scheduled Tribes students, and post-graduate scholarships for students belonging to SCs/STs and OBCs. 15 per cent for SCs and 7.5 per cent for STs are reserved in all the technical education programmes.

For higher Education for SCs/ STs, various scholarship has been established namely, Rajiv Gandhi National Fellowship for Scheduled Castes/Scheduled Tribes, Post-Doctoral Fellowship for Scheduled Castes/Scheduled Tribes and Post-graduate scholarship for Scheduled Castes/Scheduled Tribes students in professional Courses.

Educational Profile of Weaker Sections in India

The reports of the National Commission on Scheduled Castes and Scheduled Tribes are a grim reminder that the vast majority of the Scheduled Castes and Scheduled Tribes remain poor, illiterate, lack the requisite skills for competing in the modern world, enjoy unequal access to productive resources, and remain deeply tied to land and transitional occupations which offer limited possibilities of upward mobility.[12] Education is the catalyst for upward mobility. "Higher the educational profile, higher the upward mobility," can be considered as a theory. If Scheduled Castes, Scheduled Tribes, OBCs and minorities are provided good education then the education itself may lead to their social mobility. Education can serve as catalyst for upward mobility. Table number 1 reveals that the educational profile, the literacy rate and the dropout of scheduled castes in the secondary stage of education. The drop-out rate is very alarming. The drop-out rate is still a very important aspect that needs special attention of planner and educators. If we cannot reduce the drop-out rate we will not be able to think of higher education for the scheduled castes. Education may help in reducing the poverty rate among scheduled castes. There are reservation of seats in the institution of higher learning like IITs and IIMs. But if the drop-out rate is very high they will not be able to pursue their higher education.

Table 1: The Socio-Economic and Educational Profile of Scheduled Castes and Scheduled Tribes

S. No.	Name of the State	Percentage Scheduled Caste population (1991)	Percentage SC Literate Population (1991)	Percentage SC under Poverty line (1993-94)	Dropout rates of SC at Secondary Stage (1990-91)
1	Andhra Pradesh	15.93	31.59	34.92	86.00
2	Arunachal Pradesh	0.47	57.27	—	—
3	Assam	7.40	53.94	28.96	62.42
4	Bihar	14.56	19.49	62.91	89.39
5	Goa	2.08	58.73	----	81.07
6	Gujarat	7.41	61.07	38.62	71.29
7	Haryana	19.75	39.22	35.07	78.12
8	Himachal Pradesh	25.34	53.20	27.70	67.18
9	Jammu & Kashmir	—	—	—	—
10	Karnataka	16.38	38.06	54.00	75.03
11	Kerala	9.92	79.66	34.01	51.05
12	Madhya Pradesh	14.54	35.08	55.41	61.58
13	Maharashtra	11.10	56.46	52.10	71.96
14	Manipur	2.02	56.46	—	81.70
15	Meghalaya	0.51	44.27	—	30.57
16	Mizoram	0.10	77.92	—	—
17	Nagaland	—	—	—	—
18	Orissa	16.20	36.78	48.20	81.54
19	Punjab	28.31	41.09	25.02	79.34
20	Rajasthan	17.29	26.29	43.50	82.07
21	Sikkim	5.93	51.03	----	91.51
22	Tamil Nadu	19.18	46.74	52.77	77.32
23	Tripura	16.36	56.66	----	87.29
24	Uttar Pradesh	21.04	26.85	58.50	72.20
25	West Bengal	23.62	42.21	41.51	88.81
26	Delhi	19.05	57.60	---	65.36

Source: Sixth Report of National Commission for Scheduled Castes and Scheduled Tribes, 1999-2000 & 2000-2001 New Delhi, p. 40, 41, 172-4,177

Education plays a vital role in the development of individual's personality. Education is the catalyst for profile development of any individual. In our Indian society, education plays a much more role in helping the individual acquire self-esteem. Denying education to an individual, therefore, amounts to denying him/her the basic source for self-esteem and dignity. Today scheduled castes, scheduled tribes and other backward classes students are still segregated from the rest and mistreated by the upper castes teachers.[13] Calling caste names, verbal abuse and assorted humiliation acts are common practice in many schools. This may be reason for high dropout rates among scheduled Castes and scheduled tribes.

Table 2: Trends in Literacy Rates for the Non SC/ST and the population, 1961-2001

Year	*Non SC / ST*	*SC*	*GAP**
1961	27.91	10.27	17.64
1971	33.80	14.67	19.13
1981	41.30	21.38	19.13
1991	57.69	37.41	20.28
2001	68.81	54.70	14.11

Source: The Census of India, 1961 – 2001.

* Percentage point difference between the Non- SC/ST and the SC population.

The table number two reveals the fact that the literacy rate for the Scheduled Castes, Scheduled Tribes from 1961 to 2001 there is a 14 per cent gap. There is a significant gap between the SCs/STs and non-SCs and STs. Non SCs/STs are the OBCs. Their education has been deprived by the upper castes. The education of SCs and STs is not constant. It goes up and down in these five census records.

Table 3: Literacy Rates for the Non SC/ST and SC Populations by Sex and Rural and Urban Situation, 2001

Residence	*Total*	*Male*	*Female*	*M/F Gap*
	Non SC / ST Population			
Total	68.8	78.7	58.2	20.50
Rural	62.6	74.3	50.1	24.20
Urban	81.8	87.6	75.3	12.30
Urban-Rural Gap	19.2	13.3	25.2	
	SC Population			
	Total	**Male**	**Female**	**M/F Gap**
Total	54.7	66.6	41.9	24.70
Rural	51.2	63.7	37.8	25.90

Urban	68.1	77.9	57.5	20.40
Urban-Rural Gap	16.9	14.2	19.7	
Non SC/ST – SC Gap				
Total	14.1	12.1	16.3	
Rural	11.4	10.6	12.3	
Urban	13.7	9.7	17.8	

Source: Census of India, 2001.

One feature common to both in SCs and STs is the internal gap between genders. In case of SCs, the gender gap is about 24 per cent. In comparison with the non-SCs and STs counterpart the SC female lag behind by 16.3 per cent. Few girls manage to get literacy.

Table 4: Educational Attainment by Age and Levels for Social Groups, 2001

	SC Population					
Levels of Education	***7-9***	***10-14***	***15-19***	***20-24***	***25+***	***All ages***
Literate without Formal education	1.2	1.1	2.5	4.1	7.0	4.10
Up to Primary	98.80	87.5	41.0	37.3	49.5	61.2
Middle	0	10.4	30.2	22.4	17.2	16.3
Secondary	0	0	20.8	17.0	13.5	10.4
Higher Secondary	0	0	5.2	12.5	5.9	4.5
Under Graduate	0	0	0.2	1	0.6	0.4
Technical Diploma	0	0	0	0.1	0	0
Non-technical Diploma	0	0	0.2	0.9	0.6	0.4
Gradate & Above	0	0	0	5.7	6.3	3.1
All Literate & Educated	68.00	78.50	73.50	63.00	39.60	54.70
Non SC /ST Population						
Literate without Formal education	1.18	1.1	1.5	3.25	4.47	3.36
Up to Primary	98.81	84.07	29.95	27.2	36.64	49.54
Middle	0	14.82	28.82	18.66	16.11	16.21
Secondary	0	0	29.07	20.09	18.5	15.12
Higher Secondary	0	0	9.59	17.82	9.99	7.32
Under Graduate	0	0	0.41	1.49	1.24	0.8
Technical Diploma	0	0	0.04	0.13	0.12	0.08
Non-technical Diploma	0	0	0.37	1.36	1.12	0.72
Gradate & Above	0	0	0	11.47	12.72	7.64
All Literate & Educated	73.22	83.86	82.12	77.17	62.74	68.8

Source: Census of India, 2001.

When one sees the technical education for SCs it is abysmal nil. Even the graduation level shows very negligible. The contrast between the non-SCs/STs population may not necessarily seem to be striking because a huge chunk of population of OBC category gets dissolved into much more striking visible contrast of the non-OBC upper caste population in terms of education. Now there is a move to reserve some seats for OBCs in the central institution. Though there is protest from the upper caste.

Table 5: Educational Attainment for 15+ Population by Social Groups and Sex, 2001

Educational level	*Non SC / ST*		*SCs*	
	Male	***Female***	***Male***	***Female***
1. Graduate & Above	8.8	4.6	3.4	1.0
2. Graduate Degree other than Technical	68.2	67.5	69.6	70.0
3. Post Graduate Degree other than Technical	17.3	21.0	18.6	18.9
4. Technical Degrees				
(a) Engineering & Technology	8.6	4.0	5.1	3.6
(b) Medicine	2.2	1.9	1.4	2.1
(c) Agriculture & Dairying	0.4	0.1	0.3	0.1
(d) Veterinary	0.1	0.1	0.1	0.0
5. Teaching	3.3	5.5	4.4	7.1
6. Others	0.1	0.1	0.1	0.2

Source: Census of India, 2001.

At graduates the male and female difference in terms of achievement is respectively two per cent. At the same time it shows that an almost equal track record for both male and female at post graduation level. Technical degrees are important to show the difference of representation of male and female. Both SC/ST population and non-SC/ST population there exists a significant difference between male and female representations in technical education and thereby proves to be a difference between male and female in terms of professional choice which becomes clearer when it comes to teaching. The over trend in professional streamlining in itself clearly talk about the plight of the individuals according to their gender identity. Since technical degrees are undoubtedly the prime determinant deciding social as well as business opportunities, the difference between the SC/ST and the non SC/ST becomes so crucial matter to be taken note of it.

Table 6: Participation in Higher Education of the SCs 1991 and 2001

Stages of Higher Education	*Courses/ Streams*	*1991*		*2001*	
		Male	*Female*	*Male*	*Female*
Total Higher Education		9.0	4.5	11.1	8.8
Research & Post-Graduate		8.9	2.2	13.4	9.3
GraduateGeneral/non-technical Graduate		9.4	4.9	14.0	8.2
	BA/BA Honours	13.6	5.6	16.6	9.4
	B.Sc/B.Sc Honours	6.6	4.6	11.0	8.6
	B.Com/B.Com Honours	5.8	3.6	11.5	4.9
	B.Ed/B.T.	11.0	5.0	15.2	11.0
Graduate technical/Professional		6.4	6.9	7.4	13.6
	B.E./B.Sc Eng. /B.Arch	5.7	5.5	7.4	7.5
	M.B.B.S	8.9	8.1	11.0	10.8
Others		NA	NA	16.1	16.1
Post-Matric Diploma		10.9	3.8	10.6	12.2
	Polytechnic	8.7	8.5	10.2	11.4
	Teachers Training Schools	14.3	1.4	17.0	14.2
	Technical & Industrial Crafts	12.0	12.5	10.2	11.7

***Source*: Selected Educational Statistics, 1991 & 2001.**

No doubt there is gradual growth in every domain of higher education among Scheduled Castes. According to RUSA- National Higher Education Mission, 2013, the Gross Enrollment Ratio for higher education for Scheduled Castes and Scheduled Tribes has been increased. As per the RUSA report 2013, GER of boys in higher education has gone up by 13 per cent from 11.1 per cent in 2001. Similarly girls GER in 2013 has gone up by 9.00 per cent from 8.8

per cent. In Graduate and non-technical there is minimal improvement. It may be because they have realised the future prospect of these courses. In engineering and medical courses there is slight improvement in their enrollment. This decadal variation has shown that there is a very low progress in the enrollment of scheduled castes in the professional courses. With regard to male and female, there is somewhat satisfactory in the enrollment of female candidates in professional and vocational courses.

Enrolment of SCs/STs and OBCs in Higher Education

One can see the Gross Enrolment of these groups in Table number 7. The extent of higher education is generally measured by enrolment ratio in higher education. Three alternative methods are used to estimate the extent of access to higher education namely Gross Enrolment ratio (GER), Net enrolment ratio (NER) and Enrolment of Eligible ratio (EER). The GER measure the access level by taking the ratio of persons in all age group enrolled in various programmes to total population in age group of 18 to 23. The NER measures the level of enrolment for age specific groups namely those in age group of 18 to 23. While the EER measure the level of enrolment of those who completed higher secondary level education. These three concepts thus look at the access to higher education from three different angles.

Table 7: GER (18-23 years) and Inter-caste Disparities

Groups	*GER*	*NER*	*EER*
Scheduled Tribes	6.57	6.26	61.50
Scheduled Castes	6.52	6.17	51.21
Other Backward Classes	8.77	8.13	50.05
Others	17.22	16.26	53.90
Total	**10.84**	**10.18**	**52.61**

Source: NSSO 2004-05.

For Scheduled Tribes and Scheduled Castes, GER and NER in graduation and higher degree programmes are marked lower than OBCs. Again it is noticed that OBCs in higher education enrolment are lower than others. For Scheduled Tribes, estimated EER is somewhat high, much of which could be attributed to incentives offered to them for enrolment and studies.

Table 8: Higher Education for Scheduled Castes and Scheduled Tribes 2005-06

Course	*Scheduled Castes*	*Scheduled Tribes*
Ph. D.	3629	1520
M. A.	76632	25031
M. Sc.	23087	4540
M.Com.	13395	7978
B.A. / B. A. (Hons.)	569286	210577
B. Sc. / B. Sc. (Hons.)	187971	53327
B. Com/ B. Com (Hons.)	135778	47940
B. E./ B. Sc (Engg.) B. Arch	162498	57190
M.B.B.S./Dental/Nursing/Pharmacy/ Ayurvedic/Homeopathy	44575	19316
B. Ed./ B. T.	32376	9372
Enrolment in Open University	110674	90027
Polytechnic	67587	15997
Others (not included in specific faculty)	183432	66299
Total in Higher Education	1610920	609114

Source: Ministry of Human Resource Development, Government of India, 2005-06

There is a slight improvement in the enrolment of Scheduled castes and Scheduled tribes in higher education. Table number 8 shows the faculty wise admission of Scheduled castes and Scheduled tribes in 2005-2006.

Governmental Initiatives on Education in India

The 86th amendment adds a new article 21 A to the constitution that says: "The state shall provide free and compulsory education to all children of the age of six to 14 years in such a manner as the state may, by law determine". This makes the right to education a fundamental right for the children in this age group. A new fundamental duty was added making it mandatory for all parents to send their children to school when they are six to 14 years of age. The Prime

Minister Dr. Manmohan Singh has announced that the ratio to 65:35 for 2007-09 would be applied. This means that Center would provide 65 per cent of its share and the rest of 35 per cent would be borne by States. But in 2011-12 the share of Center-State would be 50-50 ratios. States may resist a central legislation that will force them to bear the cost of education of children aged 6-14 years. But shelving the amendment, apart from the obvious moral cost of such action, keeps the state's current constitutional burden much bigger and more intractable over the age group 0-14 years.[14]

The Ministry of Human Resource Development has asked the Center to make education free for Scheduled Castes and Scheduled Tribes up to Ph.D. in a recommendation from Congress veteran Arjun Singh that can help the party renew its appeal to *dalits.* The Ministry has also demanded an annual hike of Rs. 65 lakh per district under a key provision of the flagship *Sarva Shiksha Abhiyan* (SSA), catering to remedial teaching for SC/ST students.[15] In the 2008-2009 budget the amount for *Sarva Shiksha Abhiyan* has been hiked.

On the similar line the Prime Minister Dr Manmohan Singh termed the 11th five-year plan as India's education plan. He said that over 19 per cent of the total central gross budgetary support would be spent on the sector during the plan period. He also said, "We have increased the outlay on education from 7.7 per cent in the 10th five year plan. The 11th Five-year plan presents a comprehensive strategy for strengthening the education sector concerning all segments of education pyramid. He also said that the government is committed to achieve the Millennium Development Goal (MDG) of ensuring that all kids complete primary schooling. In case of elementary education, the government would like to see universal enrollment in the six to 14 age group.[16]

According to Knowledge Commission survey only 8 per cent of India's student-population goes for higher studies. This figure is abysmally low compared with the global average of 29 per cent. Most of the educationists are aware of the poor condition of the higher education scenario in the country. In an annual seminar of the All India Universities held in the month of December 2007, most of the professors made a passing reference to the decrease in the number of students in the country willing to pursue higher studies. The former Jawaharlal Nehru University Vice Chancellor, Dr. B. B. Bhattacharya blamed the government for the decreased number of students for higher education. He also said "the country is paying for neglecting higher education for the past 20-years. The government has not been investing enough in the education sector and hence no improvement can be expected in it." According to educationists, the poor higher education graph in the country can be attributed to three things-the high dropout rate at the high school level itself, not enough colleges and universities for students to go to and the poor economic background of parents, especially in the rural areas, because of which they cannot afford to educate their children.[17] The need of the hour is to revamp the falling standard of education of Scheduled Castes and Scheduled Tribes in India. Recently the Central government announced the establishment of 200 community colleges all over the country by June 2013. The community colleges may provide vertical mobility to young generation and weaker sections in particular.

Conclusion

The survey conducted by the National University of Educational Planning and Administration (NUEPA) for Ministry of Human Resource Development shows that enrollment percent of SC and ST has not been changed till 2006, though there has been a change in the overall ranking of states on the basis of Educational Development Index.[18] Socially and economically weaker sections like Scheduled Castes, Scheduled Tribes and OBCs are finally catching up with the rest of the country on important Human Development Indices like literacy, infant mortality etc,. While India, as a whole has shown improvement on the Human Development Index during this period, weaker section, like Scheduled Castes, Scheduled Tribes and OBCs have improved at a much faster rate. The development is due to spread of education. The composite Human Development Index is composed of three indices-health, income and education. The education has shown maximum improvement.[19] Hence, education must not be considered as trade but as a service. The service to weaker sections that were debarred from learning for centuries should be the focus of government. Good education generates knowledge and today globalisation process is both education-driven and technology-driven. It was education only, which made Dr. B.R. Ambedkar what he was. Similarly, the Christian missionaries in general and the Society of Jesus in form of Jesuits Fathers in worldwide particular, had changed the world by establishing and running high quality educational institutions, authentic centers of excellence, to say the least.

Endnotes

1. *Bharatatil Aspustahncha Prashna,* (Marathi). S.M. Mate wrote this book in 1930. There were many leaders, social reformers inside and out side who spoke about the status of untouchables in their own way. They also tried to bring political awareness among the dalit during the freedom struggle.

   Also see in details, Joseph Benjamin, 1989, "Leadership for Political Awakening for depressed Classes", *Third Concept*, February, 1989.
2. P.N. Prabhu, *Report of the Seminar on casteism and removal of Untouchability* (Bombay: Published by India Conference of Social Work, 1955), p. 104.
3. G. Hanumantha Rao, Caste and Poverty: A case study of Scheduled Castes in a delta village (Mulikipuram: Savithri Publication, 1977), p. 254.
4. Vithal Ramji Shinde established the depressed Class Mission in Bombay in 1906.
5. H.R. Isaacs, India's Ex-Untouchables, Bombay: Asia Publishing House, 1965, p. 41.
6. D. Keer, Ambedkar Life and Mission, Bombay: Popular Prakashan, 1962, pp. 301-02.
7. Dr. Babasaheb Ambedkar, *Yanche Bahishkruit Bharat ani Muknayak* (Marathi), Education Department, Government of Maharashtra, 1990, pp. 194-98.
8. See detail in Ambedkar's *Writing and Speeches*, Vol. 9, Education Department, Government of Maharashtra.
9. Op. cit., Ambedkar, *Bahishkruit Bharat.*
10. Gopal Guru, "The Politics of Naming" *Seminar* 471, November 1998, p. 16.

11. Now new term has been emerged as *dalit* Brahmins. Mayawati tried to give reservation benefit to *dalit* Brahmins in Uttar Pradesh after her election.

12. *Seminar,* 471 Nov. 1998, p. 12, also see Joseph Benjamin, (1989), *Scheduled Castes in Indian Politics and Society*, ESS Publication, New Delhi.

13. In the early April 2007, when new school headmaster named Sharad Kaitade, an upper caste, took over the charge of *Zilla Parishad* School at Bhandara village he is allegedly performed *puja* in the school. A lady teacher named Madhavi Raut sprinkeled *gomutra (*cow urine*)* in the class and the school premises to purify the school. The students were writing their annual examination. Lady teacher asked the *dalit* students to get up and sprinkled cow urine on them saying that this would purify them. This is height of ill treatment to *dalit* in this 21st century. See "Panel to probe Bhandara purification incident," *The Times of India* (Nagpur Edition), April 27, 2007.

14. Tapas Majumdar, "Education Should Be a Right" *Times of India* (Nagpur Edition), December 14, 2007.

15. Arjun Singh wants free studies for dalits till Ph. D. *Times of India*, January 10, 2008, p. 9.

16. Prime Minister was speaking during the 20th Convocation of Goa University, "11th five-year plan to focus on education," *Times of India*, December 29, 2007.

17. Higher Education Scenario *Hitavada (*Nagpur Daily), January13, 2008.

18. *Times of India* (Nagpur Edition), January 24, 2008.

19. Ravish Tiwari and Amitabh Sinha, "Bharat catching up with India: Human Development Index" *Indian express* (Nagpur), October 22,2011.

3

Reservation for OBCs - Opening of Pandora Box

Introduction

The founding fathers of the Constitution prescribed reservation for Scheduled Castes and Scheduled Tribes. Earlier intention was political reservation of Scheduled Castes and Scheduled Tribes into Lok Sabha and Legislative Assemblies of States. Today as per the Peoples' Representation Act 2008, the SCs and STs will have 84 and 47 seats reserved in Lok Sabha respectively. Later it was extended to educational institutions and in the area of employment. The Constitution provides for enabling provisions for government to take special steps to protect and safeguard the interest of Scheduled Castes, Scheduled Tribes and Other Backward Classes. This affirmative action was to offset and overcome "capability deprivation" due to poverty and disadvantage certain sections of society endured for many centuries due to pernicious caste system.[1]

Be that as it may, the effort is being made to reserve 33 per cent seats in Lok Sabha and States Legislative Assemblies for women. The Rajya Sabha has already passed this bill amidst din and hooliganism on March 9, 2010 and now with fingers crossed one awaits for Lok Sabha to approve the bill. Now the different parties are trying to demanding seats for Muslims, *dalits* and OBCs within this quota. Democracy occasionally and tentatively attempts to redress gross injustice embedded in social structure of the country. The *quotocracy* has its own logic of mystification. It has historical context to boot. The famous French traveller to new nation America, French Politician and Political Scientist, Alexis de Tocqueville (1805-1859) said that in a democracy the myth of formal equality can disguise as substantive inequality. In a *quotocracy*, the fact that select individuals from some communities are empowered is considered as empowering the community. This mystification is justified as a compensation for democracy's mystification. In a democracy there is a gap between formal and substantive equality, and in *quotocracy* we can empower the elites within communities with impunity and call it empowerment for all.[2] Yet *quotocracy* is susceptible to new mutations later on. So the tinkering process takes the form of a new social engineering device called *quotocracy.*

The present chapter would confine to the study of reservation policy of Other Backward Classes. The study would be in three parts, viz; definition, the history of reservation, studying the *Mandal* Commission report, study the indicator of backwardness and lastly analysing the reservation policy for OBCs. The chapter would not touch the women reservation bill which is yet to be approved.

In India, reservation generally means a quota system in legislature, public services end educational institutions, fixed by the government under the constitution under-girded by rulings of the Supreme Court in favour of the deprived and disadvantaged sections of society.

Genesis of Reservation Policy

Reservation of seats was introduced first time for selected castes in Madras Presidency in 1918. Mysore Princely State was one of the Princely States that extended special facilities to backward communities with regards to education and recruitment in state services. It was done in 1921 on the basis of the Miller Committee Report, which recommended certain steps for adequate representation of non-Brahmins in the services of the state.[3] In 1927, the Madras Government classified Communal government order and earmarked separate quota for each group for recruitment to government services. In 1928, the State Committee recommended to the State of Bombay certain provisions or special facilities regarding education and recruitment in government services to the members of depressed classes, aboriginal, and hill tribes and other backward classes.[4] Dr. B.R. Ambedkar who participated in all the three Round Table Conferences as a representative of the Depressed Classes, which included all *Shudra* castes be recognised as a separate entity in the body politics of India. This was convened by the then Prime Minister of Britain Ramsay Macdonald in London during the year 1930-32. Dr. B.R. Ambedkar here advocated their cause with great vigour and force, which shocked the world and enlightened those who felt concerned for the oppressed and down trodden. However, much later he donned the mantle of drafting the Constitution of a new independent India. He defended the provision of reservation for scheduled castes and scheduled tribes, which was for a period of ten years.[5]

He said, "The demand for reservation is demand for protection against the aggressive communalism of the governing class which wants to dominate the servile classes in all fields of life." This brought into sharper focus- caste and economic development: though from the flanks the relationship between modernity and *meritocracy* would make the goal of casteless-cum-classless society more complex.

Dr Ambedkar, in a memorandum submitted to the minority committee in the Round Table Conference had demanded reservation of seats in legislature, service and appointment of an officer to ensure implementation of these rules.

The Simon Commission (1928) accepted major demands of reservation of seats for the untouchables in the legislative bodies, special educational concessions and recruitment to government posts. At the Round Table Conference in London, Dr B.R. Ambedkar demanded the inclusion of certain safeguards in the future constitution including, separate electorates, recruitment of services, laws against discrimination, and a special department to look after the Depressed classes.[6] Subsequently in the Poona Pact, which was signed on September 24, 1932, Dr Ambedkar relinquished the demand for separate electorates in return for a system of reserved seats to be elected from 'Joint' or general electorates. The Poona Pact provided 148 seats for the untouchables instead of the 78 given by the communal awards. The benefit Dr Ambedkar wrested was the compensation for the principle of separate electorate he relinquished.[7]

Leaders in the Second Round Table Conference (1930) could not arrive at an agreement especially owing to the attitude of the Congress representative Mahatma Gandhi who claimed to represent every community and group in India. As a result of this the then Prime Minister Ramsay Macdonald made his unilateral Communal Award declaration. The Communal Award contained the following provisions in respect of various communities.

The Prime Minister made it clear at the outset. 'In the statement made by the Prime Minister on 1st December last on behalf of His Majesty's Government at the close of the second session of the Round Table conference, which was immediately afterwards endorsed by both Houses of Parliament, it was made plain that if the communities in India were unable to reach a settlement acceptable to all parties on the communal question which the Conference had failed to solve His Majesty's Government were determined that India's constitutional advance should not on that account be frustrated and that they would remove this obstacle by division and applying themselves a provisional scheme. Under the communal award reservation in legislature was granted to Depressed Castes, representative of backward areas, Sikhs, Mohammedans, Indian Christians, Anglo Indians, Europeans, Commerce and Industry, Mining and planting, land holders, university and labour. Under the communal Award Moslems, Christians, Sikhs, were granted the right to elect their representatives. Even Marathas were granted seven seats reserved for them. Gandhi had no objection to that. His only objection was that the Depressed Classes should not be given separate electorates for as stated by him in his letter to Mr. Samuel Hoare the Secretary of State in India. He requested him to revoke his decision and added, "I hold that separate electorate is harmful for them and for Hinduism whatever it may be from the purely political standpoint. To appreciate the harm that separate electorate would do to them, one has to know how they are distributed amongst the so-called Caste Hindu and how dependent they are on the latter. So far as Hinduism is concerned, separate electorates would simply vivisect and disrupt it. Gandhi went on a fast unto death to coerce the Untouchable to agree to forego the rights granted under the Communal award. An agreement was ultimately signed between the leader of the Untouchables headed by Dr. Ambedkar and Mahatma Gandhi, the leader of the Hindu communities. This agreement is known as Poona Pact. Under this pact 148 seats were reserved for the Untouchables as against 78 granted under the Communal Award but the Untouchables lost a precious right.[8]

Dr. Ambedkar was appointed Chairman of the Drafting Committee and Minister of Law in the Government. For deliberations of certain important subject different committees were set up. Minorities Committee was set up under the Chairmanship of Sardar Vallabh Bhai Patel, Minister of Home in Nehru Cabinet. This Committee discussed reservation in Legislature and services.

While Christians[9] were the first to forego their concession like reservation in Legislature and services, the Sikhs were the only religious minority, which demanded the continuance of reservation made in their favour under the Communal Award and Govt. of India Act, 1935. Sikhs demanded reservation but when the Hindu members of the Constituent Assembly vehemently opposed this demand they demanded reservation in favour of the Scheduled Caste Sikhs. While Sikhs asserted there was no Untouchability among the Sikhs, the other group keeping in view the realities and the fear of the Scheduled Caste Sikhs reverting to the Hindu religion and the interests of the Sikhs as a whole insisted that they be allowed reservation in legislature end public services. Later on the Scheduled Caste Order was amended in 1956 and all castes were included in the Scheduled Castes Order. Scheduled Tribes were given these facilities under the Constitution for the first time and a separate list was appended to the Constitution.

Backward Classes and Reservation Policy

Founding fathers of the Constitution have made a provision to make a study of the difficulties of the other backward classes and then providing them relief in the form of reservation in services because some groups were not adequately represented in services and were found educationally and socially backward. In the scheme of things under the Constitution Articles 15 (4), 16 (4), 46, 338 and 340 special opportunities have been provided for scheduled castes, scheduled tribes and other backward classes. The Government of India set up first commission under the Chairmanship of Kaka Kalelkar on January 29, 1953 and submitted its report on March 30, 1955. After a detail examination of the commission's report, the government laid its copy together with memorandum of action taken before each house of the Parliament on September 3, 1956 in compliance with article 340 (3) of the constitution. In this Memorandum it was observed:

> *"For the purpose of the enquiry specially contemplated in article 340 of the constitution it was necessary to consider whether these other backward sections could be properly classified and the commission had to find objective tests and criteria by which such classification were made, they had to find indisputable yardsticks by which social and educational backwardness could be measured. The report of the commission has not been unanimous on this point, in fact; it reveals considerable divergence of opinion."*[10]

The report of the Backward Class Commission was never discussed in the Parliament. The Central Government never acted on the Commission's report and left it to the State Government to sanction such reservation. After the lapse of 26 years another commission was appointed under the chairmanship of Mr. B.P. Mandal on January 1, 1979 by a notification issued by the government of India under the order of the President. This commission emanates from article 340 of the constitution of India. It was a historic report and significantly prepared. In this report each and every point has been considered and taken care of which was not treated properly and nor was feasible to treat properly at the time by Kaka Kalelkar Commission (1953) was rejected. Rejecting the Kaka Kalelkar commission report it was said that the commission did not evolve criteria on objective test. Mandal Commission has adopted scientific method to evolve criteria for determining the definition of backwardness. It constituted an expert committee under the eminent sociologist M N Shrinivas to suggest formulas for carrying on test. Mandal in his report said that backward class constitute 52 per cent of total population, he recommended only 27 per cent reservation for their in view of the judicial pronouncements that reservations should not exceed substantially 50 per cent of services. *Mandal* Commission submitted it report on reservation for OBCs to Home Minister, Bhuta Singh on 1980. The report was opened and remained in cold storage for many years. It was V.P. Singh government, which accepted the report and took effort to implement the reservation for OBCs. During V.P. Singh government anti-*Mandal* protests engulfed India. In 1993 a case was filed in Supreme Court. There has been case Indira Sawhney Vs Union Government of India on the question of reservation for OBCs in central government jobs. The Supreme Court finally cleared all legal hurdles to its implementation. The Supreme Court for the first time defined the creamy layer and laid down the criteria for those who should be kept out of it. It decided to have two criteria, i.e., (i) those with annual family income exceeding Rs. 2.5 lakh. (ii) Class I and II government officers, MPs, MLAs and their children. It asked the government to remove the creamy layer from the OBCs list and then provide reservation to socially and educationally backward classes. In 1993 the first *Mandal* recommendation extended to all Central government jobs by V.P. Singh. The UPA (United Progressive Alliance) came in power in 2004 and the Union Minister for Human Resource Development (HRD) Arjun Singh took interest in OBCs votes and implemented the second Mandal quota in Central Educational Institutes like IITs, IIMs, NITs and central universities. Arjun Singh has done what even the original Mandal messiah V.P. Singh shied away from–carving quota out of higher education.

Backwards: Caste-Class Dilemma

On the question of 'who are backward,' there are number of cases on which Supreme Court has given its judgments. Among many cases M.R. Balaji vs State of Mysore, Justice Gajendragadkar, observed that, the backwardness under Article 15 (4) must be social and educational. It is not either social or educational. It may not be irrelevant to consider the caste of the said groups of citizens while dealing with the question as to whether any class of citizens is socially backward or not. However, though the caste may be relevant, its importance should not be exaggerated. If the classification of backward classes of citizens was based solely on the caste of citizens, it may not always be logical and may perhaps contain the voice of perpetuating the castes themselves. Moreover, if the caste of the group of the citizen is made the sole basis for determining the social backwardness of the said group, that test would inevitably break down in relation to many sections of Indian society which do not recognise castes in the conventional sense known to Hindu society (e.g. Christians or Jains or even lingayats). Hence, though caste in relation to Hindus may be a relevant factor in determining the social backwardness of groups or class of citizens, it can not be made the sole or the dominant test on that behalf. Social backwardness in the ultimate analysis is the result of poverty to a large extent.[11]

R. Chitralekha vs. State of Mysore case is only a relevant and not a compelling circumstance in asserting the backwardness of a class and where it can be done the social backwardness of a group of citizens can be determined without reference to caste at all.[12]

In the Case of State of Andhra Pradesh vs. Sagar, Justice Shah observed, "the criteria for determining the backwardness must not be based solely on religion, race, caste, sex, or place of birth and the backwardness being the social and educational must be similar to the backwardness form which Scheduled Castes and Scheduled Tribes suffer.[13] In Janaki Prasad vs. State of Jammu and Kashmir, the Supreme Court observed that social and educational backwardness is due to poverty.[14] There have been number of case which, define the finer nuances and parameters of backwardness.

Constitutional Provisions and Reservation Policy

Indian Constitution guarantees equality to all its citizens. Article 15 and 16 prohibit discrimination against any citizen on grounds only of religion, race, caste, sex, language or place of birth, whether in respect of employment or admission to educational institutions, etc. But by ensuring equality of opportunity to all citizens in respect of educational and employment opportunities, we may be ignoring the special problems of some backward sections of our Indian society who have suffered from social, cultural, educational and economic deprivation for centuries together. Article 15 (4) empowers the State to make special provision for the advancement of any Socially and educationally backward classes of citizens or for the Scheduled Castes and Scheduled Tribes. Article 16 (4) provides an exception to the general principles of non-discrimination in matters relating to employment or appointment to any office under the state embodied in article 16 (2). The article 16 (4) states:

> *"Nothing in this article shall prevent the state from making any provision for reservation of appointments or posts in favour of any backward classes which in the opinion of the state, in not adequately represented in the services under the state."*

As *Mandal* Commission says:

> *"On the face of it, the principle of equality appears very just and fair, but has a serious catch. It is a well-known dictum of social justice that there is equality only amongst equals. To treat unequal as equals is to perpetuate inequality. When we allow weak and strong to compete on an equal footing, we are loading the dice in favour of the strong and holding only a mock competition in which weaker partner is destined to failure right from the start. This approach does ensure the 'survival of the fittest', which can be regarded as the "Law of Jungle".*[15]

Justice K. Subba Rao, makes the concept of social justice much more clear in his following statement: "In a limited sense, the right to social justice may be defined as the right of the weak, aged, destitute, poor, women, children and other underprivileged persons, to the protection of the State against the ruthless competition of life. It seeks to give the necessary adventitious aids to the under privileged so that they may have the equal opportunity with the more advanced in the race of' life. It is a bundle of rights; in another sense it is carved from other rights; in another sense it is preserver of other rights. It is the balancing wheel between haves and have-nots".[16]

Dr. Ambedkar has put this principle of equality effectively. He says the objective of equality is not an equal treatment to all but creation of an equalitarian society. When all are equal, unequal treatment to a few would create inequality in society. But when there is inequality inherent in society, equal treatment to all would create obstacle in the way of creation of an egalitarian society.

Conceding the Demand for Reservation

Backward Classes are not demanding reservation in legislature but only in services. Many states have already have already introduced reservation in services. Former Human Resource Development Minister Arjun Singh has introduced reservation for Backward Classes in central educational institutions, like IITs, IIMs, and Central Universities.[17]

Muslims, and *Dalit* Christians have also been demanding reservation in services.[18] The West Bengal Government implemented the Ranganath Mishra Commission report and provided 10 per cent jobs for OBCs among Muslim. As per government's directive, the Muslims who are socially, economically and educationally backward, are to be given reservation in all government jobs.[19] Similarly the Andhra Pradesh government has also provided 4 per cent reservation in jobs and educational institutions to 15 socially and educationally backward classes among Muslims. Unfortunately the Andhra Pradesh High Court has quashed the state policy of providing reservation to Muslims. The High Court has said that religion cannot be basis for reservation. This is the third time since 2004 that the High Court has quashed a quota for Muslims.[20] Dr. Rakesh Sinha, a, Political Scientist from University of Delhi in his talk on "Wrong Consequence of Ranganath Mishra Commission" opposed the reservation based on Religion.[21] The apex court stayed implementation of Andhra Pradesh order but left it to the High Court to dispose the batch of writ petitions. The question arises if the Scheduled Castes from Hinduism, Sikhism and Buddhism are given reservation, why not *Dalit* Christians and OBCs-Muslims be given quota. In this case reservation is certainly based on religion.

While dealing with the history of reservation in services and its implementation one sees that if it had been properly and earnestly implemented a stage would have arrived that the beneficiaries themselves would have demanded its abolition. Government spends more time, money and energy on publicity than on its actual implementation.

The Union Government has told the Supreme Court that the concept of exclusion of creamy layer from the benefits of reservation cannot be applied in the elections.[22] Senior Counsel, Harish Salve, appearing for the respondent submitted before the Supreme Court that as per the Constitution, reservation is meant for a class and not a caste. He also submitted that the creamy layer among OBCs was not entitled to contest election from reserved constituencies as the reservation was meant for socially, educationally and economically backward sections of the society. Till date, the OBCs quota is applicable only in jobs and admission to educational institutions.[23]

Reservation Policy: An Electoral Ploy

After the defeat of DF (Democratic Front) government in Maharashtra in 2014 Lok Sabha election, Congress-NCP government has thought of extending reservation to Marathas and Muslims. The government has fixed the quota of 16 per cent to Marathas and 5 per to economically backward Muslims in education and government jobs. The move has come ahead of Maharashtra State assembly election to be held in the month of October 2014. The reservation policy of Maharashtra State government will benefit nearly 43 per cent of the state's population–Marathas constitute roughly 32 per cent and whereas Muslims constitutes 10. 6 per cent of State's population. The total reservation percentage in the State has gone up to 73. It is said that the state government has rejected the Maharashtra State Backward Class Commission's contention that the Marathas do not qualify for the reservation. On November 14, 2014, Bombay High Court stayed the ordinance brought in by the Congress government to provide reservation to the Maratha community in government job and educational institutions. The Supreme Court fixed the quota that reservation should not go more than 50 per cent. Many states in India have more than 25 per cent of Muslim population in their state. Still they have not reserved seats for Muslims. They are:

State-wise Muslim Population and Reservation

States	*Muslim Population*	*Reservations for Muslims*
West Bengal	25.2 per cent	No
Kerala	24.7 per cent	No
Uttar Pradesh	18.55	No
Bihar	16.55	No
Karnataka	12.2 per cent	4 per cent *
Assam	30.9 per cent	No
Andhra Pradesh	9.25	5 per cent *
Maharashtra (Proposed)	10.6 per cent	5 per cent

*Quota within existing quota, court had struck it down.

Source: Government of Maharashtra.

Claiming that 99 per cent of the former Chief Ministers of Maharashtra belong to the Maratha community, former Journalist Ketan Tirodkar has filed a PIL in Bombay High Court challenging the state Cabinet decision providing reservation for the community in job and educational institutions. Now Government of Maharashtra has come out with job reservation for constables' wards. Where will other members of State go? Is really the reservation policy going to uplift the downtrodden people of Maharashtra? Who are downtrodden people of State? Is this reservation policy of DF government going to benefit the community or will bring back DF government in power? One has mull and ponder these questions. . Yes, DF government lost the election.

Conclusion

The real answer to reservation would have been to increase the number of Indian Institute of Technologies (IITs), Indian Institute of Managements (IIMs), Central Universities and All India Institute of Medical Sciences (AIIMS). The UPA government has taken initiative and started more and more number of IITs, IIITs, NITs and Central Universities. Our political leadership has chosen to indulge in cynical vote bank politics. Expanding the base of reserved seats to unrealistic and unfair levels is a selfish ploy by a party to increase its electoral appeal irrespective of the cost to society. Sixty seven years of independence, India should ideally have less reservation, not more, where they exist, quotas must be based on economic need and not caste distinction. We must build a meritocracy, not a *caste-ocracy* society.

Dr. B.R. Ambedkar did suggest that reservation of more than 50 per cent would seem to be unreasonable. But the Supreme Court has ruled no citizen of India can claim reservation either in jobs or in admission to educational institutions as a matter of right and reservation cannot be given at the cost of efficiency in administration and governance as per Article 335 of the constitution. Justice Cyriac Joseph and Justice S.B. Sinha said that reservation is a concession given to disadvantaged class of people as per Article 15 and 16 of the Constitution but the concession cannot be given in the line with Article 335 of the Constitution which lays down that efficiency in administration and governance can not be lost sight of. They delivered judgment on the appeal of Andhra Pradesh Public Service Commission against the judgment of the A.P. High Court dated July 23, 2008 holding that reservation to Scheduled Castes, Scheduled Tribes and Other Backward Classes should be provided from the preliminary stage during recruitment in state services in group one and two categories.[24] In another judgment the Supreme Court has ruled out that providing reservation benefits to Scheduled Castes, Scheduled Tribes and Other Backward Classes candidates in the post-graduation courses is the sole discretion of the Government and a student cannot claim it as a matter of fundamental right.

A three-judge bench of Chief Justice K.G. Balakrishnan, Justice P. Santhasivam and Justice J.M. Panchal said though a preferential treatment can be given to the candidates belonging to the reserved and underprivileged communities, yet, there is no Constitutional obligation for the Government to fulfill the same.[25] Interpreting Articles 15(4) and 16(4), the Apex Court said the provisions only tells of a preferential treatment to the disadvantaged sections of the society, but does not make it mandatory. Citing its earlier rulings, the Apex Court said, Article 16(4) of the Constitution confers discretion and does not create any constitutional duty and obligation.[26] In this court judgment, it seems that reservation is not a right but it is a concession. And providing admission in PG courses cannot be taken as mandatory by the educational institution. There is a proposal to reserve jobs in the private sector for which the government is preparing to amend the Constitution. The Supreme Court judgment in the P.A. Inamdar vs State of Maharashtra case of August 2005 disallowed quotas in private institution.[27]

There has been mixed response to the question of reservation to Scheduled Castes and Scheduled Tribes and OBCs. A mechanical engineer from IIT Mumbai, Rachna Mane has said that there was recent expulsion of fifth year quota student from IIT for repeated failure. 'Imagine the humiliation,' she exclaimed. She might have not taken admission. That is why she has been against reservation. I never saw myself as inferior to anyone till I took a reserved seat in IIT. Reservation is the worst solution a civilisation can ever think of.[28] Ms. Praniti Shinde, daughter of Union Minister, Sushil Kumar Shinde, while contesting for 2009 Maharashtra State Assembly seat from Solapur on October 13, 2009, when asked about reservations, said that, "*to an extent, based solely on economic criteria, for a couple of years, I think it's okay.*" [29]

No doubt many may agree with her. For example, it is argued that caste favouratism and social exclusion is there even in blue chip and "dynamic modern sector of the Indian economy."[30] Reacting on Women's reservation Bill, BJP Rajya Sabha member Arun Shourie said that he is personally opposed to implementation of any form of reservation policy. He said that reservation system is a never ending process. After having reservation for SC/ST, OBC and Minorities, now it is turn of the Women's reservation Bill. He strongly suggests that "merit should be criterion for selection in educational institutions and job placements and not the reservation system."[31] If we provide benefits on caste basis we will go on hampering national unity due to growing misunderstanding among the people of different castes.

Marc Galanter also opined, viewing the policy of reservation on caste basis, "the little done vast undone."[32] Tavleen Singh, a Columnist, Indian Express, said that, "we must stop all reservations. They have failed as a form of affirmative action and have served mostly to create ugly little aristocracies of supposedly deprived Indians and a false sense of entitlement among those who believe that the state owes them a living." She also said that "*dalits* continue to be mostly poor and illiterate and they continue to live in ghettoes on the edge of villages across India in a form of unspoken apartheid. The situation of *Adivasis* has not improved through reservation either."[33] The Union Government has told the Supreme Court that the concept of exclusion of creamy layer from benefits of reservation cannot be applied in election.[34]

It is true that the whole family generation is being benefited by reservation policy. There are still more who are yet to get. Isn't it possible to restrict reservation to one or two family generation(s)? It is high time that policy makers should think on this line and provide reservation benefit to those who have not got yet or no one from the family has availed yet. The academicians should start a debate on the very pertinent issue of reservation in India. The reservation quota is limited but the claimants of this cake are many. Year after year the claimants are being added for creating captive vote banks.[35]

The bottom line remains that reservation as a policy instrument of the State has emancipated and empowered hitherto lower caste people during the sixty three years of Indian independence. It has set free vast swathes of people trappered in a generational cycle of social exclusion and marginalisation. But sadly speaking it has a flip side, too. The Politics of reservation has created a Frankenstein monster out of reservation policy much against the stated aims of the framer of the Constitution. It has spawned "reverse discrimination" syndrome. Ironically enough those castes who have benefited much out of the policy wish to perpetuate the system intergenerationally, so that they can go on extracting as much benefit as possible. Without donning the mantle of Cassandra one shudders to think that the entire Indian State may be swamped by tidal wave of reservation in various guises and forms. The *quotocracy* is a new mutation making waves in contemporary India. But it has been garnished with *mobocracy*. The ideal goal of government should be elimination of obnoxious concept of caste. Is it important to provide reservation to OBCs based on caste or on the basis of income? By giving reservation on the basis of caste, aren't we promoting caste system in our society? Some academicians say that caste is relevant. Imtiaz Ahmad says that backwardness very substantially arises from lack of access to economic resources and facilities like quality education and employment opportunities. He still feels that caste based reservation is relevant.[36] If caste is considered relevant, why the Government of India has decided not to include caste as one of the parameters in the 2011 census? Home Secretary Gopal K. Pillai said that "Caste will not be included in the 2011 census." Parties like PMK, RJD, JD (U) and a few others had demanded in the past inclusion of caste in the decennial census especially the survey focusing on Other Backward Castes to buttress their demand for OBC reservation. The last caste-based Census was held in 1931, but there have been sporadic calls foe one after the implementation of the Mandal Commission Report.[37]

Pradipta Chaudhary feels that reservation should be based on hard data. He said, "Caste-based reservation in education and government employment are supposed to benefit India's most deprived, but in reality they have hardened rather than eroded India's ancient system of discrimination. He also says that since India gained independence, government has systematically refused to collect sufficient data on the socio-economic aspects of caste. The huge mass of evidence available in the censuses and land revenue settlement reports from 1901 to 1931 lies ignored. If caste is a good indicator of deprivation now, it should have been even clearer in the past. But statistical analysis of this evidence–the only accessible macro-level quantitative data for the whole country–does not confirm caste as a clear indicator of deprivation.[38] Dr. Navanetham Pillay, United Nations High Commissioner for Human Rights has unambiguously stated that if insurmountable walls like slavery and apartheid have been broken down and dismantled for good, it is high time that caste a contemporary form of slavery has to be eliminated from its very foundation.[39]

Time has come for civil society activists and innumerable NGOs' to pitch in their contribution in ushering a casteless-cum-classless society. Reason for it is due to the nature of state and character of people. The Indian state is "soft" and the people are freeloaders having propensity to expect freebies. For many, reservation is a means to quickly climb-up the socio-economic leader with a yengeance, despite the fact that their condition does not warrant it. If not, caste groups arm-twist the government by resorting to physical violence and anti-social behaviour vandalism in form of torching government properties, holding *dharna*s, stopping trains etc. Aim is to paralyse the government machinery and in the end the governments gives in. This is the ugly visage of politics of reservation policy. It has generated intra-caste animosities and severely eroded the social fabric. Not only that, it has affected business and commerce and loss to national exchequer and livelihoods of many people caught in the crossfire of social unrest and law enforcement agencies efforts to contain violence. Political Parties choose candidates for election both at national and State level on criteria of caste affiliation. Individuals are nominated for canvassing and mobilising the prospective voters on basis of their clout and political weightage.

So we are in no win-win situation as the albatross of reservation policy tightening its grip over our neck is taking us to an abyss of social disintegration. It is, therefore, observed that "the worlds over, voters are being wooed with hope of change. Indian voters looking for a vision are being lived with instruments of division."[40] We have to find some alternative social mechanism to rid ourselves lock, stock and barrel before this poisonous viper aka reservation swallows us all. If more and more categories and segments of population raise the ante for reservation benefits a time would come when there would be nothing in the national cake to give even a small slice or bite to anyone. Sooner than rather later we are inching our way to the dreaded destination. The very social mindset of casteist prejudice has to be fought with hammer and tongs without any delay. Two disparate instances in two different continents substantiate this assumption. A *Dalit* man and his physically challenged daughter have been torched to death because a *dalit* and *jat* dog owners clashed in Mirchpur village in Hisar district in Haryana very recently.[41] More surprising is the opposition of high caste faculty members of Colombia University in installation of Ambedkar Chair for Studies, Research and Analysis of Indian Political Economic – in honour of the distinguished alumni of the said University.[42] We need totally a new paradigm of social change and transformation.

Endnotes

1. Jean Dreze and Amartya Sen, "India's Development and Participation" , Oxford University Press, New Delhi, 2002, p. 36.
2. Pratap Bhanu Mehta, "Our wonderful Quotocracy", *The Indian Express,* (Mumbai-Nagpur) March 15, 2010.
3. Backward Classes Commission (B.P. Mandal, Chairman) Report: Vol. I and II, New Delhi, Controller of Publications, Central Social Welfare Board, 1980, p. 5.
4. Joseph Benjamin (2010) "Reservation Policy: A Double Edged Sword" In *Social Justice, Politics and Anomie*, (Ed.) Bhawani Singh, Jaipur: Gautam Book Company, p. 32
5. Op., Cit. Joseph Benjamin, p. 31.
6. Marc Galanter, 'Competing Equalities." Delhi: Oxford University Press, 1984, p. 31.
7. *Ibid.*, p. 32.
8. Op. cit. Joseph Benjamin, p. 37.
9. Today they have been demanding reservation and wants that Ranganath Mishra Commission's report may be implemented.
10. K. Subramaniam and P.S. Verma (1982), Notes and Comments on Mandal Commission, New Delhi, Canning Lane, p. 14.
11. AIR., 1963, Supreme Court, 649, p. 659, Quoted by R.K. Paliwal, "Reservation of Backward Classes" *Meerut Journal of Political Science and Public Administration*, Vol. 6, No. 1, Jan-June 2003, p. 101.
12. A.I.R., 1964, Supreme Court, 1823. Quoted by R.K. Paliwal, "Reservation of Backward Classes" Meerut *Journal of Political Science and Public Administration*, Vol. 6, No. 1, Jan-June 2003, p. 101.

13. A.I.R., 1968, Supreme Court, 1. Quoted by R.K. Paliwal, "Reservation of Backward Classes" Meerut *Journal of Political Science and Public Administration*, Vol. 6, No. 1, Jan-June 2003, p. 101.

14. A.I.R., 1973, Supreme Court, 930. Quoted by R.K. Paliwal, "Reservation of Backward Classes" *Meerut Journal of Political Science and Public Administration*, Vol. 6, No. 1, Jan-June 2003, p. 101.

15. Untouchability, Scheduled Castes and Nation Building" by Bhagwan Das, in Scheduled Castes and the Struggle Against Inequality, (ed): Jose Kannanakil, Indian Social Institute, New Delhi, 1983, p. 21.

    Also see V.U. Bhatkar, Philosophy of Reservation, Unpublished paper, Indian Social Institute, New Delhi, 1982, p. 8.

16. *Ibid*., p. 21.

17. Shankker Aiyar with Neeraj Mishra "Casting for votes," *India Today,* May 15, 2006, p. 19.

18. Joseph Benjamin, "Dalit Christians and Human Rights," *Institute of Human Rights,* Nagpur, 2007, pp. 19-31.

19. "Bengal ready with Muslim job quota", *The Indian Express*,(Mumbai-Nagpur) Feb. 9, 2010.

20. HC quashes Andhra Pradesh on quota for Muslims," *The Indian Express*, (Mumbai-Nagpur) Feb. 9, 2010.

    Now the matter is with Supreme Court. The Bench allowed for the time being 4 per cent reservation envisaged in the Act to be extended to the 14 identified groups, excluding the category simply termed other Muslim groups. See, *The Indian Express,* (Mumbai-Nagpur) March 26, 2010, p. 1.

21. "Dr. Rakesh Sinha opposes religion-based reservation," *The Hitavada, (Nagpur Daily)* February 14, 2010.

22. "Creamy layer criteria cannot be applied for elections" *The Hitavada,* (Nagpur daily) August 23, 2009.

23. *The Hitavada,*(Nagpur daily) August 23, 2009.

24. The *Hitavada, (*Nagpur daily*)* April 21, 2009.

25. The Apex Court passed the judgment while dismissing the appeal of a medical student Gulshan Prakash and others challenging the denial of reservation benefits to SCs/STs in post-graduation courses MD/MS/PG Diploma and MDS offered by Maharshi

Dayanand University for academic session 2007-2008. See, *The Hitavada,* (Nagpur daily) Dcember 3, 2009.

26. "Reservation for SCs, STs Not mandatory in PG courses: SC" *The Hitavada, (Nagpur daily)* December 3, 2009.
27. Neeraj Mishra, "Fate Accompli" *India Today, May 15, 2006, p. 26.*
28. *Ibid.,* p. 29.
29. The *Indian Express*, (Mumbai-Nagpur) October 3, 2009, p. 1.
30. Sukhadev Thorat and Kathernie S. Newman (ed) (2010), Blocked by Caste: Economic Discrimination in Modern India, Oxford University Press, p. 48.
31. Arun Shourie was speaking in the International Conference on Environmental Health and Technology at IIT-Kanpur. See "Personally against any form of Reservation" *The Indian Express,* (Mumbai-Nagpur) March, 16, 2010.
32. Marc Galanter, Competing Equalities, Delhi: Oxford University Press, (1984) p. 567.
33. Tavleen Singh, "No more reservation" *The Indian Express,* (Mumbai-Nagpur), March 28, 2010.
34. "Creamy layer Criteria can't be applied for election: Government to SC" *The Hitavada, (Nagpur daily)August* 23, 2009.
35. Op. cit., Joseph Benjamin, Reservation Policy: Double-Edged Sword", p. 49.
36. Imtiaz Ahmad, "Caste is Relevant", *The Times of India* (Nagpur), June 25, 2007.
37. "2011 census will not be caste-based: Centre", The Hitavada (Nagpur daily) March 8, 2010.
38. Pradipta Chaudhary, "Don't Put It In A Caste," *The Times of India,* (Nagpur) June 26, 2007
39. "*People's Reporter*, Mavelikara, Kerala, October 25-November 10, 2009, p. 5.
40. *India Today*, April 12, 2010.
41. *The Times of India*, (Nagpur) April 23, 2010.
42. *Mainstream* (New Delhi) April 17, 2010.

4

Violating Children's Rights: A Blot on the Nation

Introduction

Children form one-third of India's population but their share in the Indian budgetary allocation is a mere 4.86 per cent. About 80 per cent of Indian children continue to be anaemic, 47 per cent malnourished. Infant mortality ratio has remained at 67 per 1,000 and the all India child sex ratio is 927 girls for 1,000 boys. This is the condition of our Indian children. And they are considered as future citizens of India. But before they attain full-fledged citizenship they have to face a number of problems. Some die before they become the future of Nation. For example in Mumbai, the country's financial capital, it is estimated that there are over 100,000 homeless children. If one studies the education level of children one finds that even today 3.3 per cent of children are out of school.

Unfortunately it is observed that in developing countries, most of the children do not attain their childhood. They are forced to skip their childhood. There are many factors which compel them to become adult at a very early age. Children are forced to a miserable life without even the basic necessities. As a result, most of the children fail to develop their full social and economic potentialities, which would enable them to become as a useful member of the society. How can they become the future of India?

Demographic Aspects of Child in India

India has the second largest child population in the world. According to 1991 census, the child population was 58 per cent, which accounted for over 50 per cent of the total population of the country. The child population has grown faster than the total population and its share in the country's population has increased remarkably from over 42 per cent in 1971 to 52 per cent in 1991. The age—specific sex ratio of the child population has shown a continuous increase with the increase in age. In the age group 0-14, the sex ratio has been heavily in favour of males but these have recorded a fall over the period 1907 - 1971, as is evident from the decline in the sex ratio from 120.2 in 1901 to 113.1 in 1971. In India male species is considered and treated as the first sex. The 1991 census of India shows that the sex ratio in India continues to favour men, for every 1,000 men there are 927 women. The sex ratio in India declined. In 1901 the sex ratio of females per 1,000 males was 972. In 1911 the sex ratio of females had come down. Now when we have entered 21st century the sex ratio of females has come down to 927 per 1,000 males. May be because we have adopted new technology for sex determination to identify girl baby in the mother's womb and stop her entry in this world. There is slight upward trend from 2001 and 2011 census. According to 2001 census, it was 933 per 1000 and in 2011 it is 940 per 1000.

The 2001 census figure reveals that in the 0-6 age group, the prosperous States of India viz., Delhi, Punjab, Haryana and Gujarat have the lowest sex ratio (number of girls per 1,000 boys). The most affluent pockets in some cities show the sharpest drop.[1]. With latest modern medical diagnostic input, many male members of the family indulge in foeticide with impunity. There are so many agencies working for the development of children in India. The Government of India has many plans and schemes for the welfare of children. Still some 200 million children in the third world are forced to make their own living, many of them working under slave-like conditions.

In this chapter an effort would be made to list out the various problems faced by Indian Children. Though there are so many provisions in the Indian Constitution, still the future of Indian citizen is very bleak. Many conventions have been held at the International level; still the children in India face many difficulties. From the very childhood they are trained to be "anti-social" and "notorious". A child looses his childhood and becomes a premature mother of a child. In this chapter an attempt would be made to study various conventions held on children on world forum. Effort would also be made to find out the existing constitutional provisions which are there in our constitution but the children, which are the future of India, suffer a lot. In this chapter an effort would be made to portray the problems of children in the Industrial sector. In what ways children's' rights are being violated will be studied in this chapter.

International Conventions and Child's Rights

Various meetings/parleys/conventions were held globally to save the children from exploitation. But we find that the status of children has not been improved. Their condition is worst in Asia and African continents. Poverty compels them to work in the field where as they are supposed to be in schools, they are found in garages, tea-stalls, hazardous factory etc. How can these conventions be meant for children? The basic rights of children were recognised by the international community and consequently the following United Nations' Covenants/Instruments took shape:[2]

1. Geneva Declaration of the Rights of the Child 1924
2. Convention Concerning Forced Labour 1930
3. Universal Declaration of Human Rights 1948
4. Declaration of the Rights of the Child 1959
5. UN Convention Against Torture and Forms of Cruel Inhuman or Degrading Treatment or Punishment 1987
6. Convention on the Rights of the Child 1989
7. World Declaration on the Survival, Protection, and Development of Children 1990
8. World Declaration and Agenda for Action Against Commercial Sexual Exploitation of Children 1996

All these conventions of the UN especially, deal with the problems of children of the world. Since 1924, the World body has been discussing on the problems of children but still they live in inhuman conditions in different parts of the world today. In the Universal Declaration of Human Rights, the United Nations has proclaimed that childhood is entitled to special care and assistance. In view of this, the United Nations Commission on Human Rights adopted on 20th November, 1989, the *"Convention on the Rights of the Child (CRC)"*, intended to promote and protect the well-being of children, in the General Assembly. The CRC was ratified by India in December, 1992. Till date, 191 countries have signed the CRC (Somalia and the US being the exceptions.). Comprising 54 Articles, the CRC, which treats all human beings, below the 18 years as children, draws attention essentially to four *sets of rights* for every child, namely:

1. **The right to survival**: Includes the right to a life with dignity, right to an attainable standard of health, nutrition, and an adequate standard of living, and the right to a name and nationality. These rights seek to ensure that children have nutritious food, potable drinking water, a secure home and access to health facilities.
2. **The right to protection** : Includes freedom from all forms of exploitation, abuse and inhuman or degrading treatment. This includes the right to special protection in situations of emergency and armed conflict. The aim is to protect vulnerable children from those who would take advantage of them and to safeguard their minds and bodies with proper custody and care.
3. **The right to development** : This right accords the child the right to be educated, to receive support for development and care during early childhood, right to social security, leisure, recreation and cultural activities. This right also seeks to ensure that children can practice their own religion and culture.
4. **The right to participation** : Includes right to appropriate information, freedom of thought and expression, conscience and religion, and right to an independent view on matters. The aim here is to ensure that children are able to develop their own set of values and principles and that they have the opportunity to freely express themselves and their opinions.

The rights of the child enshrined in the Convention on the Rights of the Child (CRC) can be classified into two categories, namely:

(a) **Immediate rights**: They include rights against discrimination, punishment, and the right to fair hearing in criminal cases and a separate system of criminal justice, right to life, right to nationality, right to re-unification with the family and protection rights. These rights must be guaranteed by every country on an immediate basis.

(b) **Progressive rights**: They include health and education rights which are not covered by the first category. CRC recognises them as *economic, social and cultural rights*, which the countries are expected to ensure over a period of time, in view of the lack of resources available with the country immediately.

Indian Constitution and Child Rights

Several Articles of the Indian constitution deal with Children's Rights in India. [3]

More Prominent among them are:

Article	*Constitutional Provisions*
Article 5	Right to Citizenship
Article 14	Right to equality before law.
Article 15 (1)	Prohibits state from discrimination on the grounds of religion, caste, sex, and place of birth.
Article 15 (3)	Special provisions may be made by state for women and children.
Article 19 (1)	Guarantee of six freedoms (speech, assembly, association, movement, residence and profession).
Article 21	No deprivation of life or personal liberty. Except according to procedure established by law.
Article 22	Ensures safeguards upon arrest and deals with preventive detention.
Article 23 (1)	Prohibition on human trafficking, forced labour, beggary etc.
Article 24	Prohibits employment of children below 14 years.
Article 25 (1)	Right to freedom of conscience, freedom to profess, practice and propagate religion.
Article 28 (1)	No religious instruction in institutions wholly funded by the State.
Article 29	Guarantees cultural and educational rights to religious and linguistic minorities.

Article 32 (1)	Guarantees the right to move the Supreme Court for enforcement of fundamental rights.
Article 226	Guarantees the right to move the High Court for enforcement of fundamental rights.
Article 39	Requires the state to direct its policy towards ensuring means of livelihood without exploitation.
Article 41	Requires the state to make provision to secure right to work, education and public assistance.
Article 44	Requires the state to make efforts for a uniform civil code.
Article 45	Requires the state to make efforts for free and compulsory education till the age of 14 years.
Article 47	Requires the state to increase the level of nutrition, and standard of living, to bring about prohibition.
Article 51	Requires the state to foster respect for international law and treaty obligations.
Article 350	Requires the state to ensure that linguistic minorities receive primary education in mother tongue.

By the 86th Constitutional Act, 2002, the right to education of children has been made a fundamental right in Chapter III. The Constitutional Amendment Act, 2002 provides for insertion of a new Article 21 A that the State shall provide free and compulsory education to all children of the age of six to fourteen years in such manner as the state may, by law, determine. (See Right to Education Act, 2009)

Besides constitutional provisions, there are various policies formulated by the government of India as well as the States, *viz*: (I) National Policy for Children, 1974: The National Policy for Children, 1974 (NPC) states that 'children shall be protected against neglect, cruelty and exploitation. To achieve the above aims, the state shall provide necessary legislative and administrative support. (II) The National Policy on Education, 1986: The NPE, among other things recommends 'firm exclusion of corporal punishment in schools. However, the state governments are yet to amend State Education Acts and Rules to ban corporal punishment in schools. In the next part of this chapter I would discuss the problems of Indian Children.

Child Labour

The Employment of Children Act of 1938 and the Article 24 of the Indian Constitution prohibits children from working in hazardous industry. Even on November 20, 1989 the UN promulgated the convention of the Rights of Children's. Signatory states promised to recognise the right of children to protection from economic exploitation. But who respects the UN charter. Who honours the Indian Constitutional provisional? Are these to be studied or to be practiced?

There are many surveys made which show that many children are employed in hazardous industries / factories. The UN report has pointed out that one million children are being forcibly taken from India to neighboring countries and 7000 from Nepal into the country, thus earning the perpetrators 32 billion dollars every year.[4]

The National sample survey estimated it at 17.36 million based on its definition of child workers as a person below the age of 14 who is a wage earner.[5] From the low-wage labour of these children, some of them are also as young as five. The work that is imposed upon a child is often dictated by the needs of his family, under exploitative conditions that call for greater physical and mental resources than the child possesses. This is the way the child labour has been defined in the Indian context. If we look at the figure in the developing continues, we find that children under age 15 make eighty per cent of all Pakistani carpets. Few of them make the legally required minimum wage; many fall a prey to sickness by the wool dust. Children in India, Nepal and Afghanistan too make rugs in order to survive. Children pick up tobacco leaves in Indonesia, tea leaves in Sri Lanka, oranges in Brazil.[6] Children of Bangladesh cut coca beans without knowing the taste of chocolate. In Thailand, children mostly make handbags. They cut diamonds in the Indian slums and comb throughout Egypt's jasmine fields starting before sunrise.[7]

According to ILO report, there are about two hundred million children under age 15 who earn their livelihood. The London Human Rights Organisation, Anti-Slavery International estimates that there are eight million children who are forced to do slave labour in the

Andes, hundreds of thousands are working off their parent's debts on Brazilian plantations and thousands of others are servants in South African households.

The UNICEF study has pointed out that our 11 million children are in bondage with the tally excluding street children and those employed in domestic labour who constitute another half a million.

In the Indian situation, child labour is not a new phenomenon. It existed in one form or the other since historical time in all the societies of the world. It is only in the late 60s that people started perceiving it as social problem. In the olden days the school-based education was confined only to the privileged children acquired in the family and through their hard work. Agriculture and art-culture-based craft and trade were all family enterprises and the child participated in them as a helper or an apprentice. During this time, the child worked under the direct guidance of his parents or master-craftsman and therefore, his work was a sort of vocational training. Such work did not deprive him of his physical and mental growth; rather it inculcated in him a positive self-image by preparing him to assume the role of an adult in future.

With increasing modernisation and urbanisation the whole social scenario has changed. The industrial revolution created such vast demands for job that even compelled the children to look for job. The exploitative nature of the elite societies compelled children to work in factory, canteen, motor-mechanic workshop, match-factory etc. Earlier, the work that was done by the child to learn something under the protection of his parents now had to be done for his family's sheer survival without enjoying the benevolent protection of his guardians. Many a times, he has to work at a distance, quite far from his home and is treated in an inhuman way.

Mirzapur carpets are famous. What is swept under their delicate intricate designs is that they have been woven for a pittance by eight year-old children in dark, cramped condition, Subhadra Sen Gupta[8] had explained the inhuman condition of Mirzapur carpet weaver. He narrates that the whole system is organised to exploit the children to the maximum. He says most of the children working in carpet industries in the areas around Varanasi, in Khamaria, Auraii, Gopigunj and in the districts of Mirzapur are brought here by recruiting agents from the nearby tribal areas of Bihar like Sitamarhi and Palamau. Their parents are usually landless labourers to whom these agents loan money and then coerce the boys to go and work at the carpet looms. The children are taken away from their parents, so that they can exploit more and they cannot easily run away from the industry. One carpet is sold for Rs. 100-400 and child worker is paid Rs.5-10 per carpet. If one sees their wages, there are no set wage patterns; it is just a verbal agreement with the boy. Some boys work on *dhurrie*. The *dhurrie* looms need to be laid flat on the ground. They are usually set-up outside. These boys work outside in 40°C in the afternoon sun with a hot dusty wind blowing. They have no adequate cover against the sun. Why do children do these types of activities then? It is all because they do not know the curse of their illiteracy. Whether they work in the canteen, or a motor mechanic's workshop, for them it is an advantage to work instead of labouring in the fields. If the *malik* (owner) of various workshops were happy, they would give some money to watch a film. For them, it may be joyful moment for these children. But many a time these children do not understand the exploitative nature of *malik*.

Over a 100 million children around the world, mainly in Asian countries, are working in terrible conditions at appallingly hazardous jobs for a pittance. In India alone some 5.5 crore children are forced to sell their childhood and future for livelihood.[9] At the Firozabad glass factories, the state industry at Mandsaur, Colombian brick works, Egyptian tanneries, Delhi canteen workers, Delhi motor mechanic workshop and Peruvian mines are few areas where one can find child workers.

In all these areas, mostly male child is preferred. These child workers in their early age look like 20-year adult workers.[10] He skips his childhood. Their face shows that they are doing the job that they should not have done otherwise. These children have always a feeling of insecurity of their job and that is why they are more submissive and easily exploited. Their life is always in a total darkness. No one has little time to sit and ask the problem of the child who has served them in various ways.

Girl Children and their Position

In India, the male species is considered and treated as the first sex. The 1991 census of India shows that the sex ratio in India continues to favour men, for every 1,000 men there are 927 women. The matter of India's missing women has raised concern since the abnormal female-deficit population sex ratio first noted in 1971 census. Since then the ratio has grown almost steadily more masculine, despite small upswings in proportion to female in 1981 and 2001.Though India's 2001 Census shows a 6-point increase in the population sex ratio to females per 1000 males (927 F/1000 M in 1971), this still shows a substantial female deficit.[11] This would again come down if government does not put complete halt on technology to identify baby girl in mother's womb. All over country Amniocentesis is being used to discover the gender of the unborn child, and if it is a girl, abortion follows. A glaring example of this practice was found in Bombay where in 1984. 40,000 female foetus were aborted. In one hospital, a study showed that out of 8,000 abortions performed, 7,999 were female. Families who were unaware of these type of instruments and could not kill the unborn child, start killing the girl in different ways when they are grown up. From foeticide to infanticide, from lack of health care and nutrition to illiteracy, from early marriage and too many pregnancies after rape and dowry deaths, the female population in India lives by sufferance.

What is the main reason for this discrimination? Why they are neglected and kept aloof from the mainstream of our society. It is all because the girls are considered as child bearers. It has been reported that in India, every year 12 million girls are born. One and a half million die before their first birthday, another 8, 50.000 before their fifth, and by the 15th year only 9 million will survive with or without sufferings.

The National Policy of education (1986) put more emphasis on the education of girls. It is aimed at removing traditional discrimination and sex stereo typing by diversifying school curricula and promoting the access of girls to vocational and professional courses. After four decades of independence, it has been observed that women are still fully dependent on the male counterpart. In many families it is considered that sending girl child to school is a sheer waste of money, it is because girls are treated as temporary guests in their own house. They think that after all girls have to go to their in-laws house and would confine themselves to kitchen work. They cannot do anything other than kitchen work. In most of the families, the male child is given higher education, good care, good food, etc. In India, between the age of 5 and 9 there are 44.33 per cent of male children who attend school. Among girls, the percentage is well below, i.e. 32.21 per cent.

In the age group of 10 to 14, it has been found that 62.07 per cent boys attend school. In comparison to boys; there are only 37.47 per cent girls who continue their studies. If we take up the state-wise percentage of children attending schools, one can find that Kerala is the only state where the percentage of children attending schools is much higher than any state in India. While comparing the boy and girl, children attending the school at the age of 5-9, it reveals that the percentage of these two is almost same i.e., 75.14 boys and 75.06 girls.[12] But now it is claimed that in some districts of Kerala there is 100 per cent literacy. In Maharashtra over one lakh children continue to remain out of school even after the implementation of *Sarva Shiksha Abhiyan* which suffers due to under utilisation of fund poor infrastructure at schools. (*Times of India* 30/4/2007, Between 2001-2005 only Rs 911.37 Cr was available with Maharashtra Prathamik Shan Parishad against approved Rs 2,155.87 Cr.)

Rajasthan is one of the states where the percentage of girls attending schools is extremely low. In comparison between boys and girls age 10-14 it shows that 58.84 per cent boys go to school, where as only 18.68 per cent girls are sent to school. Most of the girls are asked to stay at home and learn the house-work and prepare themselves to become good house-wives. It has also been observed that girls are meant to work in the kitchen. In Bihar there are around 24 *lakhs* children between six and 14 years who do not go to school. An effort is made with the help of Bihar Police to put child labour in to the school. This campaign has been on for about a month now and 20, 000 odd new students have already been added to the rolls of government primary schools.[13]

Girl-Child Mother

The State of Kerala claims 100 per cent literacy. Do literate people favour child marriage? A perusal of the records of the district hospital at Manjeri and a few schools in the district and interviews with a cross-section of the teachers, advocates, marriage brokers, gynaecologists and family counselors and women activists give the disturbing fact that more than 60 per cent of the girls in the districts, belonging to different religions are married off even before they are 18, some even before they attain puberty. of this, not less than 90 per cent become mothers within one or two years. This record also reveals that 70 girls aged 18 or below gave birth to children during January-February 1994. Child mother is the happiest sign for the old parents. They like to see their grand and great grand children before they leave this world forever. The record of school shows that every girl is married at the age of 12-15 while she is still in school. In this process marriage broker are trying to solemnise the marriage at the earliest possible. Nair family in this district prefers marriage at the age of 15-20.[14] Among Muslim families, it would be difficult to get a suitable partner for a girl after post graduation.

A survey conducted by the family counselling centre in the Melappuram municipality found that, in a single ward, 18 divorced women in 20-35 age group are without any children. This is in the state of Kerala where literacy rate is high. This can also be found in other states. Rajasthan is the state where child marriage is very common. In their young age they become mother and skip teen-age-hood. That is why the female mortality rate is high in Rajasthan. The nexus between marriage and literacy is poignantly brought out by the fact that Kerala has the highest female literacy (75 per cent), while Rajasthan has 18 per cent. This direct link between the two factors has other implications; later marriage means later pregnancy, fewer children and higher life expectancy rate. When one takes into account the fact that 13 per cent of female deaths before 24 are due to pregnancy and childbirth complications, the importance of literacy in this area becomes very clear. If the child-mother's husband is dead, then she has to sit on the pyre with her husband. Religious and custom sanctioned the cruelest practices such as "*sati*" human sacrifices, *devdasi* system and polygamy.

The report of National Family Health Survey III conducted in 2005-2006 reveals that that nearly 45 per cent women in India are between 20 to 24 years. It is also reported that they were married before they could attain the age of 18 years which is the legal age for marriage for girls. The number easily crosses 50 per cent in eight states of India. Around 61 per cent of women in Jharkhand were married off before 18 years of age. The statistic shows that in Bihar 60 per cent, in Rajasthan 57 per cent, in Andhra Pradesh 55 per cent, in Madhya Pradesh, West Bengal and Uttar Pradesh the per cent age goes to 50 per cent, and in Chatishgarh it goes to 52 percent age. This is due to the lack of education and poverty. It was found that about 71 per cent women who married below 18 years of age had not received any education.

The another survey of National Family Health Survey conducted during 1998-99 reveals that six states- namely Arunachal Pradesh, Punjab, Mizoram, Sikkim, Tripura and West Bengal had reported a lower percentage of under 18 years old marriage among women. In these six state girls marry at the age of 15 years.

Table 1: Rising U-18 Marriages

State	*NFHS II*	*NFHS III*
Arunachal Pradesh	27.6 per cent	40.6 per cent
Punjab	11.6 per cent	19.4 per cent
Mizoram	11.6 per cent	20.6 per cent
Sikkim	22.3 per cent	30.1 per cent
Tripura	37.7 per cent	41.0 per cent
West Bengal	45.9 per cent	53.3 per cent

Source: *Times of India*: (Nagpur) February 23, 2007. p. 7.

Victimisation nexus Mid-night Children

Adults, police, traders etc victimise many children living on the streets. A UNESCO sponsored census has revealed that six out of every 10 street children in Bombay city are engaged in rag picking. Among the others, only one out of every 10 is engaged in a skilled trade. One out of every seven children has taken to begging, while one out of six has drifted to manual labour.[15] A study conducted in 1989 by a Voluntary organisation, *Society for Prevention of Area Resources center* (Bombay based) has revealed that most of the street children were in the age group of 16-20. While one-third were in the 11-15 age group, only eight per cent were in the 6-10 age group and only seven children were below five years.[16] Many children spend their night on the pavement, railway platforms. Who are these children? They are child labourers, working whole day in the canteen; motor mechanics etc. and again they might have run away from their homes. Primarily, they do not find enough accommodation in their own house. Secondly, they do not earn sufficiently to hire a room. This is the tragedy of Indian children. It is an irony that some people have built good rooms for dogs and domestic animals while the future of India that is the children, have no room at all to spend a night in.

According to a survey made by the Institute of Psychological and Educational Research (1989-90), there are more than 4 Lakh Street children in the four metropolises of India.[17] The sociologists say that the street children are mainly from migrant families or orphans, abandoned or runaways. In India, house is a very big problem for people living in cities. In cities, all the members of family cannot live in one small room or a small hut. Some spend nights on the pavement or railway platforms.

Today after six decades of independence about 60 per cent people are living in either hut or mud-house. In rural areas, at least two-third population of India lives in this type of house. There are people who are without any house. Many people leave their native places and come to cities in search of job. With the small amount, they cannot afford to live in a good house and also use good water. They are compelled to live in a slum and use contaminated water. *Dharavi* in Bombay is considered the biggest slum area in Asia. These 175 hectares of land comprise Asia's largest slum. *Dharavi* is situated in a low-lying area, which is affected by floods in every monsoon. Since *Dharavi* slum area is small and population is more people prefer to spend nights on the roadside and railway platforms.

The adult and male child of the family can spend nights on the roadside. What about to those female children who just cannot spend night on the roadside because of the fear of rape.[18] And as a result, in their childhood, the female child becomes the mother of a child. The future of Nation is real dim.

Child Prostitution

The problem of child prostitution exists in almost all Asian countries. Tourists visiting these countries for sex come from developed nations. The children get the dreaded disease from their customers and then pass it to others.[19] At the Madras medical college, the largest maternity hospital in Asia, adolescent pregnancies are no longer a surprise.[20] During the last six years, the number of teenage pregnancies have accounted for nearly 10 per cent of all the cases and average around 1.600 a year.[21] At the Government Kasturba Gandhi Hospital, the other large maternity hospital in Madras, teenage pregnancies have been common. Here the abortion rate is much higher among teenagers. A majority of these teenagers are unmarried. These teenagers are sometime unaware of physical contact and become the victim of rape. Sometime, the girl child is given false promises and finally conceives. Most of the times many adults prefer to rape the minor girl. These girl-children are mostly from low-income group. Today's teenager is exposed to TV programmes on romance and sex on various channels. There are such parents who do allow their girls to go to a disco. While some of the girls have got involved with boys of their choice, it is pathetic to find some who are forced to undergo a sexual relationship with older men in the family and finally loose childhood and attain motherhood. Indian Express reports that a four-year-old girl was carried away by two drunken youths on September 9, 1992.

She was thrashed with an iron rod. The adults raped the unconscious child. Her mother found her child naked body sandwiched between the two youths, who were fast asleep.[22] The rising cases of paedophilia (rape of children below 10 years) have been alarming. According to a study conducted by the National Crime Records Bureau (NCRB), Uttar Pradesh recorded the maximum number of cases 546 in 1991. Madhya Pradesh accounted for 232 cases. Interestingly the Union territories of India had low incidence of such cases.[23] Many cases of rape go unreported. These cases are revealed only when the girl gets pregnant. There are many laws, acts etc. against rape of woman. Child rape is not really a problem of law and order alone but it is an aspect of moral degradation, which can be directly traced to the growing slums, which are breeding grounds for such offences. In the past three years 492 child rape cases were reported. And the majority of them took place in *Jhuggies* and resettlement colonies.[24]

According to the National Crime Records Bureau's (NCRB)[25] latest figure (1992), 10,827 women were raped in India in 1992, up from 10,410 in 1991. Child rape is up by 278 per cent from 394 in 1990 to 1,099 in 1991. And these cases are still pending in the courts. It is stated that in India a woman is raped every 54 minutes. Sexual crimes are on the rise in our cities. *India Today* reports that 54 women are raped every day in India that is one every 35 minutes! 85 percent of the rape victims are raped by men known to them.[26]

According to a well-known psychologist, "Rape is the ultimate violation of a woman's dignity. And the rape of a child is absolutely shattering for her at a tender age. The traumatic experience invariably causes irreparable physical and psychological damage". The Voluntary Organisations are doing a lot to rehabilitate these children who have been reported. Even when a child is raped, neither parents nor child would be able to reveal the facts. Since her pathetic story has not been heard, her remaining life starts as a prostitute. And that becomes her permanent shelter and business for her livelihood.

Conclusion

To overcome this problem it would be appropriate to make schooling up to standard tenth free and compulsory. If possible, the girl students can be given free education up to standards XII. In the rural areas, the children should be given mid-day meal. There are some States who are doing so like Tamil Nadu and Andhra Pradesh. Now Right to Education Act 2009 is a positive step in this direction Children can have free education with free mid-day meal. In this way, the eldest child of the family need not go to work to supplement the income of his parents. Sometimes there are so many children in one family. Many parents are not able to feed these children. Children are compelled to leave schooling and earn for house. The Government should seriously think on family planning. Those who do not follow must not be given government concession and facilities. Non-formal education can be of good help for educating the Indian mass. For this task, students, teachers can be involved. They contact the parents of bonded labour, prostitute etc. Local voluntary bodies are doing a lot for community development. There can be some more voluntary bodies health centre, community centre, playground for children, children's library, so that the children can go and spend some time in these places. Small scale Industry should be started in order to train children and employ them. They can learn so many things in these industries. Even the girl children can be given some training so that they can stand on their own feet. And in this way they can lighten the burden of family. They need not go for prostitution. In the school and college constitution law, moral and sex education should be made compulsory. Equality is to be promoted in the families and school. In the schools and colleges, there can be one preliminary paper on Child Labour Act, Child Marriage Act, Dowry Prohibition Act, etc.

Government can institute a special court to settle child marriage. Child Labour and girl Child prostitutes cases. This can be in each and every city/town/villages of India. In every city /town/*panchayat*, there can be health center exclusively for children. There should be free check-up camps in every *panchayat*. In order to encourage the voluntary bodies, government can constitute an award for their excellent work in protecting the rights of children. It is the duty of all individual to make all children, the future of Nation. If a country is to thrive and prosper in all spheres of human activity, the country has to form a policy for the welfare and development of children.

Yet, there is lot of scope for more and more NGOs to contribute their mite in the amelioration and emancipation of children from the clutches of exploitative employees and assortment of anti-social elements. Thanks to Government of India's initiative to draft a new legislation to protect the child's rights. For detail see appendix. The

Act will also tackle unlawful sexual contact, using children for begging abduction and wrongful detention, using children for pornography, corporal punishment, ragging, and intimidation intoxicating children abetting and involving children in armed conflict. Let's hope that this Act will bring some radical change in the condition of children in India. It also needs to change the people's mind-set. I mean people should take up this problem seriously. Multi-media both print and electronic could be harnessed to raise funds within the country. A multi-pronged strategy on war footing is the need of the hour.

Endnotes

1. Shefalee Vasudev, "Missing Girl Child" *India Today*, November, 10, 2003, p. 14.
2. See John Menachery, Child's Rights, Unpublished paper presented in the Matru Sewa Institute of Social Work Nagpur 3-4 March 2007 on "Human Rights and Duties".
3. See Indian Constitution chapter III basically fundamental Rights.
4. *Hitavada*, 26/2/2007 Nagpur.
5. "A country where 5.5 Cr. Kids are forced to sell their childhood" *Indian Express* (Nagpur), April 8, 1994.
6. Joseph Benjamin. 1990. "Child Labour. The quest for socio-economic inquiry" *Third concept* (New Delhi), December 1990, pp. 33-36.
7. Malappuram.. a paradise for child marriages" *Indian Express,* (Nagpur) March 12, 1994.
8. "Malappuram.. a paradise for child marriages" *Indian Express,* (Nagpur) March 12, 1994.
9. *Ibid.*
10. *Ibid.*
11. "Community living for street kids." *Times of India* (Bombay), March 18, 1989.
12. "Malappuram.. a paradise for child marriages" *Indian Express,* (Nagpur) March 12, 1994.
13. In Bihar, Cops herding kids to school, *Times of India*, March 7, 2007.

14. "Malappuram.. a paradise for child marriages" *Indian Express,* (Nagpur) March 12, 1994.
15. "Community living for street kids." *Times of India*. March 18,1989.
16. "Children of the lesser God". *Hitavada* (Nagpur), December 27, 1992.
17. "Be-Aabaru-Hoti Auratein- Bihar." *India Today* November 4, 1998.
18. "Child Prostitution on rise in Asia". *Hitavada* (Nagpur), June 24, 1993.
19. "An early burden". *Indian Express* (Nagpur), December 12, 1993.
20. *Ibid.*
21. "Lost Horizon". *Indian Express* (Nagpur), August 15, 1993.
22. *Ibid., Indian Express* (Nagpur), August 15, 1993.
23. *Ibid.,* Indian Express.
24. Rohit Brynath "The second Rape" *India Today*, February 15, 1994, p. 120.
25. Shefalee Vasudev and Methil Renuka "Rape!" *India Today*, September 9, 2002, p. 50.
26. *Ibid.,* September 9, 2002, p. 50.

5

Poverty and Malnutrition: A Matter of Concern

Introduction

Just after the World War-II, the poverty of poor people has become matter of grave concern for almost all countries of the world. After independence the Indian government undertook massive efforts to eradicate poverty from India. Even at the United Nations Millennium Summit in 2000, around 189 world leaders promised to end poverty by 2015 and agreed to set targets-called the Millennium Development Goals to reduce poverty and hunger. In 2008 world leaders decided to meet in New York to assess how far member nations have been able to full fill the goal by 2015. Poverty is the pros and con of malnutrition in India. Malnutrition refers to the lack of needed foods including protein and vitamins. It is somewhat very close to hunger. According to UN body FAO, International Fund for Agriculture Development and World Food Programme report of 2014, the number of hungry people in India has come down by 9.5 per cent to 190.7 million 2012-2014 from 210.8 million during 1990-92. India and neighboring nations are lagging behind in achieving the Millennium Development Goal of halving hunger by 2015. The hunger refers to malnutrition or outright under-nourishment—a lack of calories. In 2001, there were 830 million malnourished people in the world. This includes around 200 million children. India has 49 per cent of world's underweight children. An effort has to be done by all nations to alleviate poverty from the world. This chapter would be an effort to analyse the poverty-torn situation in India. This chapter would study sociological and anthropological concern of Indian society. Malnutrition is the effect of poverty. There is a nexus between poverty and malnutrition. This chapter will be an effort to study the correlation between poverty and malnutrition.

Poverty is an umbrella word used to describe the condition under which poor people live. Yet it is an ever-evolving concept. A poor person is one who does not have an adequate supply of food and clothing or as good housing as the average person in his own neighborhood, region, or country. Unfortunately, it is not an economic abstraction and it is a human condition. Some sociologist consider that poverty breeds poverty. Children of poor have a good chance of remaining poor all their life time. They are born losers.

Poverty is a situation that gives rise to a feeling of acute discrimination, as what one has and what one "should have." Though it has to be conceded that one should have an internal construct; hence each person's feeling and experience of poverty is individual and unique. However, all poor people possess the feeling of powerlessness and destitution. Poverty can be defined as a social phenomenon in which a section of the society is unable to fulfill even its basic necessities of life. When a substantial segment of a society is deprived of the minimum level of living and continues at a bare subsistence level, that society is said to be plagued with mass poverty.

There is an effort in all definitions of poverty to approach the average level of living in a society and as such these definitions reflect the existence of inequalities in a society and the extent to which different societies are prepared to tolerate them. For instance, in India, the generally accepted definition of poverty emphasises minimum level of living rather than a reasonable level of living.

This attitude is borne out of a realisation that it would not be possible to provide even a minimum quantum of basic need for some decades and, therefore, to talk about a reasonable level of living or good life may appear to be wishful thinking at the present of alleviating poverty may become prohibitive as the vision of a good life widens. The upshot of the entire argument is that the absolute standard of poverty expressed in terms of minimum requirement of cereals, pulses, milk, vegetables, butter or calorie intake is conditioned by the relative levels of living prevalent in the country'. Boyd-Orr, the first Director-general of FAO an affiliate of UNO was the first person to propound the notion of the starvation line in 1945, which referred to the consumption of less than 2300 calories per person per day. This idea has been transformed into the poverty line. The World Development Report 1990 supplements a consumption based poverty measure with other, such as nutrition life expectancy, under 5 mortality, and school enrolment rates. There are different theories of poverty. They are:

Ojha's view of Poverty

Mr. P.D. Ojha estimated the number of persons below the poverty line on the basis of an average calorie intake of 2,250 per capita per day. This entailed monthly per capita consumption expenditure of Rs. 15-18 (1960-61 prices) in the urban areas and of Rs. 8-11 in rural areas. On this basis, Ojha estimated that 184 million persons in the rural areas (15.8 per cent of total rural population) and 6 million persons in the urban areas (7.6 per cent of urban population) lived below the poverty line. For the country as a whole, 190 million persons (44 per cent of total population) could as poor in 1960-61.

For 1967-68, Ojha estimated that 289 million persons (70 per cent of the rural population) lived below poverty line.[1] Dr V.M. Dandekar and Mr. Nilkantha Rath estimated the value of the diet with 2,250 calories as the desired minimum level of nutrition. They suggested that whereas the Planning Commission accepts Rs. 20 per capita per month (or Rs 240 per annum) as the minimum desirable standard, it would not be fair to used this figure for both the urban and the rural areas. Dandekar and Rath, therefore, suggested somewhat lower minimum for rural population, i.e., Rs 180 per capita per annum and a somewhat higher minimum Rs 270 per capita per annum for the urban population at 1960-61 prices. However, at 1968-

69 prices, the corresponding figures for the rural and urban population work out to be Rs. 324 and Rs. 486 per capita per annum respectively.

P.K. Bardhan considered Rs. 15 at 1960-61 prices to be the national minimum as it was a conservative approximation to the minimum standard fixed by the Planning Commission's Study. Bardhan's study brought out the conclusion the percentage of rural people below the poverty line as defined above has gone up from 38 per cent in 1960-61 to 54 per cent in 1968-69.

Montek Singh Ahluwalia's Study of Rural Poverty (1977)

Montek Singh Ahluwalia studied the trends in incidence of rural poverty in India for the period 1956-57 to 1973-74. He used the same concept of poverty line i.e., an expenditure level of Rs. 15 in 1960-61 prices for rural areas and Rs. 20 per person for urban areas.

The most important feature of Montek Singh Ahluwalia's study is the marked fluctuation over time in the extent or incidence of rural poverty. The proportion of rural poverty declined initially from over 50 per cent in the mid-fifties to around 40 per cent in 1960-61, rose sharply through the mid-sixties, reaching a peak in 1967-68, and then declined again.

He, therefore, concludes: "The Indian experience over the past two decades cannot be characterised as showing a trend increase in the incidence of poverty in India as a whole. In general, the time series shows a pattern of fluctuation with the incidence of poverty falling in periods of good agricultural performance and rising in periods of poor performance."[2]

Be that as it may there are economists of diverse shades of hue and colour like Mahbub-al-Haque and Amartya Sen who view poverty from a different perspective. It has an embedded view that total quality of life is to be taken into consideration in any serious study of cause and effect of poverty.

Table 1: Percentage and number of persons living in poverty: Rural India

	No. of persons in lakhs			*Poverty Ratio (% of Population)*			*Poverty Reduction*	
	1987-88	*1993-94*	*1999-00*	*1987-88*	*1993-94*	*1999-00*	*87-88 to 93-94*	*93-94 to 99-00*
All India	3070.5	3203.7	2602.5	38.9	36.0	26.1	2.9	9.9
1. Delhi	10.3	15.5	11.5	12.4	14.7	8.2	–2.3	6.5
2. Punjab	25.2	25.1	14.5	13.2	11.8	6.2	1.4	5.6
3. Chandigarh	0.8	0.8	0.5	14.7	11.4	5.7	3.3	5.7
4. Himachal Pradesh	7.5	15.9	5.1	15.5	28.4	7.6	–12.9	20.8
5. Daman & Diu	—	0.2	0.1	—	15.8	4.4	—	11.4
6. Haryana	25.4	43.9	17.3	16.6	25.1	8.7	–8.5	16.4
7. Jammu & Kashmir	17.0	20.9	3.5	23.8	25.2	3.5	–1.4	21.7
8. Goa	3.0	1.9	0.7	24.5	14.9	4.4	9.6	10.5
9. Andhra Pradesh	160.4	154.0	119.0	25.9	22.2	15.8	3.7	12.1
10. Kerala	88.5	76.6	41.0	31.8	25.4	12.7	6.4	6.3
11. Mizoram	1.7	1.9	1.8	27.5	25.7	19.5	1.8	6.2
12. Manipur	5.3	6.8	7.2	31.4	33.8	28.5	–2.4	5.3
13. Gujarat	122.4	105.2	67.9	31.5	24.2	14.1	7.3	6.8
14. Meghalaya	5.5	7.4	8.2	33.9	37.9	33.9	–4.0	4.0

(Cont...)

15. Nagaland	3.7	5.1	5.5	34.4	37.9	32.7	–3.5	5.2
16. Lakshwdeep	0.2	0.1	0.1	35.0	25.0	15.6	10.0	9.4
17. Rajasthan	142.9	128.5	81.8	35.2	27.4	15.3	7.8	7.5
18. Sikkim	1.4	1.8	2.1	36.1	41.4	36.6	–5.3	4.8
19. Tripura	8.8	11.8	13.0	35.2	39.1	34.4	–3.9	4.7
20. Assam	75.8	96.4	94.6	36.2	40.9	36.1	–4.7	4.8
21. Arunachal Pradesh	2.8	3.7	4.0	36.2	39.4	33.5	–3.2	3.3
22. Karnataka	158.6	156.5	104.4	37.5	33.2	20.2	4.2	13.2
23. Maharashtra*	296.3	305.2	228.0	40.4	36.9	25.0	3.5	11.9
24. Uttar Pradesh	536.5	604.5	529.9	41.5	40.9	31.2	0.6	9.7
25. Pondichery	3.1	3.3	2.4	41.5	37.4	21.7	4.1	15.7
26. Madhya Pradesh	264.3	298.5	298.5	43.1	42.5	37.4	0.6	5.1
27. Andaman & Nicobar	1.1	1.1	0.8	43.9	34.5	21.0	9.4	13.5
28. Tamil Nadu	231.1	202.1	130.5	43.4	35.0	21.1	8.4	13.9
29. West Bengal	283.6	254.6	213.5	44.7	35.7	27.0	9.0	8.7
30. Bihar	420.9	493.4	425.6	52.1	55.0	42.6	–2.9	12.4
31. Orissa	165.9	160.6	169.1	55.6	48.6	47.1	7.0	1.5
32. Dadra & Nagar Haveli	0.8	0.8	0.3	67.1	50.8	17.1	16.3	33.7

Source: Compiled form M. Ahluwalia, The Journal of Development Studies (1977) and B.S. Minhas, Planning and the Poor.

* In Maharashtra over 1/5th of urban families live below poverty line (*Times of India* 24/01/2008)

The all-India evidence reveals that the incidence of rural poverty in inversely related to agricultural performance measured in terms of agricultural NDP per rural person. In other words, rising agricultural productivity per person tends to reduce incidence of poverty.

Estimate of Poverty by the Seventh Finance Commission (1978)

The Seventh Finance Commission made an attempt to have a more inclusive concept of poverty line. The NSS data cover only household consumer expenditure. In order to get a more inclusive measure of welfare or deprivation, an estimate of the benefit of public expenditure was added to private consumer expenditure norm for calculating "the augmented poverty line". To the per capita monthly private consumer expenditure norm is added the per capita monthly public expenditure by each state government under the following heads of expenditure in 1970-71: (i) Health and family planning; (ii) water supply and sanitation; (iii) education; (iv) administration of police, jails and courts; (v) roads; and (vi) social welfare. To this norm, i.e., the State Specific Poverty Lines, the maximum per capita monthly public expenditure for any state in India in 1970-71 was added. This modified State-specific norm was named as "Augmented Poverty Line".

From the data it was revealed that 277 million persons lived below the augmented poverty line in 1970-71. As a percentage of population of the 15 State, the people below the poverty line constituted 52 per cent. Out of these 225 million persons in the rural areas and 52 million persons in the urban areas lived below the poverty line. As per the Millennium Development Goals report (2008) India has 456 million people who live on less than $ 1.25 per day and India has among the highest child malnutrition in the world. (See *Indian Express* September '14, 2008.)

From the Seventh Finance Commission (1978) data, the following distinctive features emerge:

(i) As compared to all the earlier studies, the proportion of population living below augmented poverty line indicates a relatively higher figure of 52 per cent.

(ii) The proportion of persons below the poverty line in the rural and urban areas is nearly the same. This is also in sharp contrast to the conclusions of earlier studies.

World Bank and International Monetary Fund view of Poverty

The Bretton Woods twins World Bank and International Monetary Fund has some unique views of it on poverty and so the realm of developmental economics which came as a result of it. The World Bank in its country study India: Poverty, Employment and Social Services (1989) also made use of the same procedure as adopted by the Planning Commission. The poverty line is the expenditure level at which a minimum calorie intake and indispensable non-food purchases are assured. The Planning Commission for rural and urban areas defined poverty lines of Rs. 49.1 and Rs. 56.6 per capita per month for 1973-74. The World Bank used an alternative method of estimating poverty proportions applying a deflator series developed by the NSS and the Indian Statistical Institute to calculate updated poverty lines (in current prices) of Rs. 55.2 (rural) and Rs. 68.6 (urban) for 1977-78 and Rs. 89.0 (rural) and Rs. 112.2 (urban) for 1983. The World Bank also worked out the estimate of ultra-poor reckoned at 75 per cent of the expenditure of poverty line. On this basis the proportion of population below poverty line for 1970, 1983 and 1988 has been worked out.

1. The proportion of population below poverty line in rural areas declined from 53 per cent in 1970 to 44.9 per cent by 1983 – a decline by about 8 per cent during 1970 and 1983 and it is estimated to have fallen further by about 3 per cent by 1988 and stands at about 42 per cent. However, in absolute terms, the number of rural poor was about 237 million in 1970 and it rose to 252 million in 1983 and around the same in 1988.
2. The proportion of population below poverty line in urban areas was 45.5 per cert on 1970; it declined to 36.4 per cent in 1983 and further fell to 33.6 per cent in 1988. In other words, poverty percentage among the urban poor fell by about 12 per cent during 1970 and 1988. Nonetheless, the absolute number of urban poor grew by 28 per cent (i.e. from 50.5 million to 64.6 million) during 1970-83 and further by 8 per cent (i.e. from 64.6 million to 70.1 million) during 1983-88.

3. The overall percentage of the poor fell from 52.4 per cent in 1970 to 40 percent in 1988. However, in absolute terms, their number increased from 287 million in 1970 to 322 million in 1988- an increase of about 12 per cent (Refer table 2).
4. The proportion of ultra-poor in India, which stood around 30 per cent in 1970, has also declined to about 19 per cent in 1988. However, the proportion of ultra-poor for the rural areas was 20.4 per cent and that for the urban areas was 15.8 per cent. In absolute terms, it was paradoxical to find that the rural ultra-poor who number 134.6 million in 1970 declined to 123.6 million in 1988, but the urban ultra-poor increased from 28.4 million in 1970 to 32.9 million in 1988.
5. Scheduled Castes and Scheduled Tribes accounted for a third of the poor and 38 per cent of the ultra-poor in rural areas, but only 13 per cent in urban areas (15 per cent of the ultra-poor).

No doubt, the World Bank Report has brought out a profile of poverty over the 18 years period and in this sense, it gave us an indication of the trend over tow decade, but the 1988 figures have been derived on the basis of the growth rate in various states and India as a whole, assuming that growth is neutral so far as distribution is concerned. Obviously, the 1988 figures may be treated as less variable.

Table 2: Poverty in India 1938 Poverty line = Rs 89.00

State	*Urban*		*Rural*		*Total*	
	Po	***PI***	***Po***	***PI***	***Po***	***PI***
Andhra Pradesh	30.81	1.49	30.32	7.20	30.44	7.27
Assam	34.29	7.34	42.44	8.44	41.58	8.32
Bihar	49.28	14.58	62.48	19.10	60.76	18.52
Gujarat	40.05	8.79	44.43	10.28	43.04	9.81
Haryana	26.93	5.93	20.14	3.86	21.69	4.33
Himachal Pradesh	17.58	3.89	29.79	5.77	28.85	5.62
Jammu & Kashmir	39.78	7.73	14.00	1.87	19.56	3.14
Karnataka	38.6	11.33	47.88	14.53	45.11	13.57
Kerala	37.76	10.42	39.07	9.85	38.82	9.96
Madhaya Pradesh	42.06	10.41	41.71	11.01	41.78	10.88

(Cont...)

Maharashtra	38.82	11.68	50.71	14.70	46.45	13.62
Manipur	31.79	6.91	30.56	5.53	30.93	5.94
Meghalaya	11.09	1.72	44.79	14.23	38.44	11.87
Orissa	37.29	9.24	57.74	17.79	55.16	16.71
Punjab	30.96	7.51	14.72	2.51	19.35	3.94
Rajasthan	37.90	9.83	32.37	8.45	33.58	8.75
Tamil Nadu	46.80	14.21	54.06	17.52	51.63	16.41
Tripura	32.39	8.38	35.33	7.68	35.01	7.76
Uttar Pradesh	44.19	12.17	40.85	10.58	41.48	10.88
West Bengal	40.82	11.56	59.34	20.39	54.37	18.02
All India	40.03	10.94	45.07	12.70	43.90	12.29
Population-weighted co-efficent of variation	13.46	20.47	26.92	38.21	32.05	33.68

The Planning Commission

The Planning Commission constituted in September 1989 an Expert Group' to consider methodological and computation aspects of estimation of proportion and number of poor in India. Prof. D.T. Lakdawala was Chairman of the Expert Group. The Report of the Expert Group was submitted in July 1993.

Table 3: Poverty Line with base 1773-74 Rs. Per capita per month

Year	*Rural*	*Urban*
1973-74	49.09	56.96
1977-78	56.84	72.50
1983	89.45	117.64
1987-88	115.43	165.58

Source: Planning Commission (1993 report of Expert group, p. 36).

Table 4: Population below poverty line

Year	*In millions*			*Percentage of total population*		
	Rural	*Urban*	*Total*	*Rural*	*Urban*	*Total*
1973-74	261.3	60.3	321.6	56.4	49.2	54.9
1977-78	264.3	67.7	332.0	53.1	47.4	51.8
1983	251.7	75.3	327.0	45.6	42.2	44.8
1987-88	229.4	83.3	312.7	39.1	40.1	39.3

Source: Compiled from the Planning Commission (1993) Report of the Expert Group.

Taking into account various consideration, the Expert Group recommended the following criteria for determining the Poverty Line:

1. The Poverty Liner recommended by the Task: Force on projection of minimum needs and effective consumption demand, namely a monthly per capita total expenditure of 49.09 (rural) and Rs. 56.64 (urban) rounded respectively to Rs. 49 and Rs. 57 at all-India level at 1973-74 prices be adopted as the base line. This was anchored in the recommended per capita daily intake of 2,400 calories in rural areas with reference to the consumption pattern as obtained in 1973-74. The Expert group recommended that these norms may be adopted uniformly for al states.

Summary of the Various Estimates of Poverty

B.S. Minhas has indicated that the percentage of the rural poor declined during the period 1956-57 to 1967-68. On the other hand, P.D. Ojha and Pranab K. Bardhan indicate the increasing proportion of the rural poor. In their view, the direction of change indicates a trend of growing pauperisation. Dandekar and Rath have shown a constant proportion of both the rural and the urban poor during the period 1960-61 and 1967-68. However, in their estimate there is an absolute increase in the rural poor from 135 million to 166 million and in the urban poor form 42 million to 49 million. Montek Ahluwalia believes that Indian experience over the past two decades dose not indicate trend increase in poverty. In general, a pattern of fluctuation with the incidence of rural poverty falling in periods of good agricultural performance and rising in period of poor performance has been observed. The Seventh Finance Commission estimated the total number of persons living below the poverty line to be 277 million in 1970-74. Out of them, 225 million belonged to the rural areas and 52 million to the urban areas.

V.M. Dandekar estimated that in 1983-84, a total of 286 million (44.4 per cent) persons were living below the poverty line.

More recent evidence by the World Bank supports the view that the proportion of persons below the poverty line has come down from 52.4 per cent in 1970 to 42.5 per cent in 1983 and further to 39.6 per cent in 1988. Gaurav Datt and Martin Ravallion also estimate that person below the poverty line are 43.9 per cent– 40 per cent in urban and 45 per cent in rural areas.

Gaurav Datt and Martin Ravallion clearly bring out that poverty gap in rural area is 12.7 per cent and in urban areas is 10.94 per cent. Obviously, greater effort is needed to reduce poverty gap by having specific programmed for rural areas to alleviate poverty.

B.S. Minhas, L.R. Jain and S.D. Tendulkar in their study revealed that the incidence of poverty in 1987-88 at the all-India level comes to about 44.8 and 36.5 per cent respectively in rural and urban India, rather than 32.7 and 19.4 per cent as reported by the Planning Commission. For the Indian Union as a whole, it works out to 42.7 per cent for 1987-88 as against 29.2 per cent reported by the Planning Commission. In absolute terms 361 million were counted as poor in 1987-88 - 284 million in the rural areas and 77 million in the urban areas.

Planning Commission Expert Group (1993) estimated that rural poverty ratio has declined from 56.4 per cent in 1973-74 to 39.1 per cent in 1987-88. As against it, there is a relatively smaller decline in urban poverty ratio, which has come down from 49.2 per cent in 1973-74 to 40.1 per cent in 1987-88. The overall poverty ratio has, therefore, declined from 54.9 per cent in 1973-74 to 39.3 per cent in 1987-88.

Table 5: All India Estimate of Poverty Incidence

	Year	*Percentage of people below the poverty line*		
		Rural	*Urban*	*Combined (R and U)*
1. Minhas et al with appropriate price adjustment	1970-71	57.3	45.9	55.1
	1983	49.0	38.3	46.5
	1987-88	44.9	36.5	42.7
2. Planning Commission	1983	40.4	28.1	37.4
	1987-88	32.7	19.4	29.2

Source: Economic and Political Weekly, July 6-13, 1991.

Economists may have differences in methodology and thus than estimates may vary in magnitude. But there is a general consensus on two things: firstly, percentage of population below the poverty line has started declining as a consequence of the indirect benefit of higher growth rate and also as a result of the impact of the direct programmes of poverty alleviation. Still the proportion of population below the poverty line is about 37 per cent as per the Seventh Plan, which can be considered to be high. Secondly, the absolute number of the poor has certainly increased over the year.

This present graph reveals how there has been decline of poverty in India. The graph gives the status of poverty from 1973 to 2000. It has declined from 54 to 26 per cent. Let's see how far we are to achieve Millennium Development Goals (MDGs) in 2015.

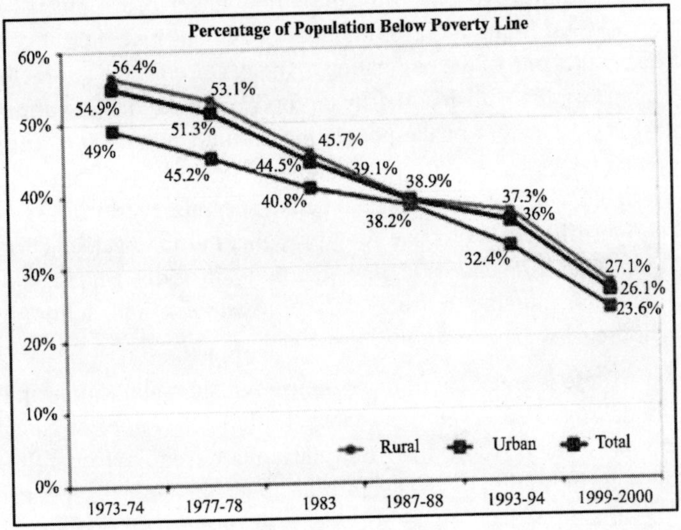

Riding on the better social indicators like health and primary health, India has achieved an over 27 per cent decline in poverty and is well on track to meet the target set for 2015 according to the United Nations. The annual report, a yardstick for measuring the achievement of the Millennium Development Goals (MDGs), predicted that higher food prices might push 100 million people deeper into poverty. According to the report, there has been a strong and sustained progress in reducing extreme poverty. But improved estimates of poverty from the World Bank show that the number of poor in the developing world is larger than previously thought, at 1.4 billion people. But the new estimates confirm that between 1990 and 2005, the number of people living in extreme poverty fell by over 400 million, and that the 1990 global poverty rate is likely to fall by targeted 50 per cent by 2015.[3]

Malnutrition in India

In the second part of this chapter, I would deal with problem of malnutrition in India. The food problem in India is a problem of nutrition. Malnutrition refers to the lack of needed foods including protein and vitamins. It is somewhat very close to hunger. The hunger refers to malnurtrition or outright under-nourishment—a lack of calories. Many Indians do not afford to nutritive diet, it is due to heavy pressure of the population in India. Once again I quote Sir John Boyd Orr, the British authority on food, observed that in normal time about 30 per cent of the population do not get enough to eat while much larger section of the population have to be satisfied almost in variable with ill-balance diet containing cereals, sugar, root vegetable and insufficient protective food of higher nutritive value. This leads to ill-health disease and high mortality in India among children, pregnant, nursing mothers, factory workers and school going children.

There is an extent of under-nutrition[4] and malnutrition[5] in India. Madalgi[6] has observed, "If we take the deficiency of calorie intake of 15 per cent or more than the nutritionally required quantity as a definite indication of under-nutrition about one-tenth (9.2 per cent) of the urban population and 40.3 per cent of the rural population was under-nourished in 1959-60, the all India average being 35.0 per cent." The majority of the under-nourished are also mal-nourished. Some 250-30 million of India's population are either under-nourished or mal-nourished or both.[7]

It varies from 22 to 55 in rural and between 21 to 38 per cent in the urban areas. In other words about 7 per cent people were subsisting on just one meal a day and another 29 per cent has to go without meal every alternate day. There were several surveys made to find out the poor condition of Indian dietaries. All gave different results. The average calorie intake amounted to 2,560 calories per consumption unit per day. In 92 surveys, the calorie intake was between 2,300-3000 calories and in 28 surveys it was 3,000-4300 calories while 17 surveys had recorded intake of 1,100-1,500. The lowest intake was recorded in survey in Kerala and highest in the Punjab. About 70-80 per cent of calories, and in some instances more were derived from cereals and pulses. The figures for fat intake were available in 127 surveys showed an amount of 23.5 gm per consumption unit per day.[8] As per the latest survey of Integrated Child Development Scheme 2014, around 11 per cent of children are underweight in Maharashtra.

An analysis of the peasant and working class dietary in different parts of India reveals that their diet was usually lacking in calories, it is ill balanced and bulky.[9] The Indian normal male spends a net of 493 Kcl. (2MJ) of energy; and a female a net of 368 Kcl. (1.5 MJ) of energy. Besides, energy is also spent for daily activities, and this has been estimated at 1220 Kcl. (4.9 MJ) for a male and 826 Kcl. (3.3 MJ) for a female. Additional calories are also needed for the performance of daily work.[10] The ICMR has recommended the energy requirement for Indians.

Table 6: Composition of on Average Diet and its approximate nutritive value

Food	*Calories*			*Proteins in grms.*		
	1951-1952	*1955-1956*	*1960-1961*	*1951-1952*	*1955-1956*	*1960-1961*
Cereals	1089	1215	1348	25.3	27.8	31.0
Pulses	175	206	214	11.2	13.2	13.7
Roots & Tubers	25	27	28	0.4	0.4	0.5
Sugar	140	130	143	0.4	0.4	0.4
Nuts and Seeds	23	17	16	0.7	0.5	0.5
Fish	3	3	4	0.4	0.6	0.6
Oils	70	73	86	0.0	0.0	0.0
Grand Total	1523	1755	1839	38.4	44.5	46.7
Milk	108	115	116	4.8	5.0	5.0

Source: Nutrition Value of Indian Foods, p. 40.

Table 7: Daily Allowance of Nutrients for Indians (Recommended by the Nutrition Expert Group in 1968)

Group	Particulars	Calories	Proteins (gm.)	Calcium (gm.)	Iron (mg.)	Vitamin A Ratinol or	Carotene	Thiamene (gm.)	Riboflavin (mg.)	Nicotinic acid (mg.)	Ascorbic acid (mg.)	Folic acid (mg.)	Vitamin B12 (kg.)	Vitamin D (I.U.)
1	2	3	4	5	6	7	8	9	10	11	12	13	14	15
Man	Sedentary work	2400		0.4 to				1.2	1.3	16				
	Moderate work	2800	55	0.5	20	750	3000	1.4	1.5	19	50	100	1	
	Heavy work	3900						2.0	2.2	26				
Woman	Sedentary work	1900						1.0	1.0	13				
	Moderate work	2200	45	0.4 to	30	750	3000	1.1	1.2	15	50	100	1	
	Heavy work	3000		0.5				1.5	1.7	20				
	Pregnancy	+300	+ 10		40	750	3000	+0.2	0.2	+2	50	150-300		
	Lactation (upto1year)	+700	+ 20	1.0	30	1150	4600	+0.4	+ 0.4	+5	80	150	1.5	
Infants	0-6 months	120/kg.	2.31/8 kg.	--	10.mg.	400	--							
				0.5							30	25	0.2	200
	7 - 12 months	100/kg.	1.81.5/kg.	.0.6	--	300	1200							
Children	1 year		17											
	2 year	1200	18		15 - 20	250	1000	0.6	0.7	8				
	3 year		20	0.4										
	4 - 6 years	1500	22	to		300	1200	0.8	0.8	10				
	6 - 9 years	1800	23	0.5		400	1600	0.9	1.0	12	30 to 50	50 to 100	0.5 to 1.0	
	10 - 12 years	2100	41			600	2400	1.0	1.2	14				
Adolescents	13 - 15 years :			0.6 to	25									
	Boys	2500	55	0.7	35	750	3000	1.3	1.4	17				
	Girls	2200	50					1.1	1.2	14				
	16 - 18 years :			0.5 to	25									
	Boys	3000	60	0.6	35	750	3000	1.5	1.7	21				
	Girls	2000	50					1.1	1.2	14				

Source: Mamoria,C.B. "Social Problems and Social Disorganisation, Kitab Mahal, p.533.

Food deficiency may cause well-recognised deficiency diseases, which do not invariably cause actual death or infirmity, but certainly leads to general-ill health and greatly increase susceptibility to many other diseases. Many surveys have been made on the effect of malnutrition. Malnutrition raises death rate in two ways. In the first place it gives rise to certain deficiency diseases and secondly it lowers the resistance power of the people some 18,000 children die every day because of hunger and malnutrition and 850 million people go to bed every night with empty stomachs, a terrible indictment of the world in 2007, the head of the UN Food Agency said. "Hunger Kills 18,000 kids every day"[11] James Morris said that while the percentage of people who are hungry and malnourished has decreased from a fifth of the world's population to a sixth of the population, the actual number of hungry people is growing by about five million people a year because of the rising population.

Today 850 million people are hungry and malnourished. Over half of them are children. 18,000 kids die every day because of hungry and malnourished. Morris said the largest number of malnutrition children is in India-more than 100 million-following by nearly 40m in China.

It is also reported that nearly half of the children in India are malnourished, putting the country in the same league as some of the world's poorest countries even though fewer infants dying and more pregnant Indian women are seeing doctors according to government data.[12] There is a very close link between poverty and malnutrition in India. It is poverty that leads to malnutrition and malnutrition leads to diseases, ill health and consequently this ultimately the result is death. In order to overcome with the problem of malnutrition the first step that government has to take is to remove poverty. Poverty is the major cause of malnutrition. The NGOs and social activists should come forward to ameliorate poverty from India. Indian government has already passed food security bill in parliament. The issue of food security is central to the pursuit of poverty eradication.

The poverty eradication is possible as it is mentioned in the recent UN report. According to the United Nations report there is decline in poverty in the world. While most of the decline in East Asia, particularly China, other regions had much smaller decreases in the poverty rate and only modest falls in the number of poor.[13] As of 2001 there were 830 million malnourished people in the world. This includes around 200 million children. India has 49 per cent of world's underweight children. An effort has to be done by all nations to alleviate poverty from the world. It has been the first Millennium Development Goals before the whole nations. All nations should join hands in removing poverty by 2015. This may also lead to malnutrition free India.

References

Minhas B.S., Jain L.R. and Tendulkar S.D. Declining incidence of Poverty in 1980s, *EPW* July 6-13, 1991.

Bardhan, P. K. On the incidence of Poverty in rural India *EPW*, Annual Number Feb. 1973.

Dandekar V.M. and N. Rath Poverty in India, dimensions and Trende *EPW* January 2,1971 and January 9, 1971.

Footnotes

1. P.D. Ojha, Configuration of Indian Poetry-Inequality and Levels of Living, Challenges of Poverty in India, p. 40.
2. Montek Singh Ahluwalia Rural Poverty and Agricultural Performance in India. The Journal of Development Studies, 1977, p.319.
3. *Indian Express*, September 12, 2008, p. 8.
4. Under-nutrition means as an inadequacy in calorie intake which if allowed to continue for a long time results in either loss of normal body weight for the same physical activities or reduction in physical activity for the same body weight or both.
5. Malnutrition refers' to lack or inadequacy of a particular or several essential such that if made good, the signs of specific deficiency diseases are eliminated.
6. See Madalgi, S.S. Population and food supply in India, 1970, p. 68.
7. Sukhatme, P.V. Feeding India's Growing Millions, 1965, p. 75.

8. See Mamoria, C.M. Social Problem and Social Disorganisation, Kitab Mahal, New Delhi, p. 528.
9. Mukerjee, R.K. Food Planning for millions 1938, pp. 78-80.
10. A physiological calorie [also called kilocalorie or Kcl] is the amount of heat necessary to raise the temperature of one Kg. of water by one degree centigrade. Now the unit Joule is used instead of calorie for expression of energy values. The new units kilojoules (KJ) and Megajoule (MJ) are used for expressing the energy of foodstuffs. 1Kilocalori=4.184 kilojoules (KJ) or 4,184 Joules. 100 Kilocalories=4.184 Megajoules (KJ).
11. *Times of India,* (Nagpur) 19/2/2007. p. 11.
12. *Times of India*, (Nagpur) Feb. 11, 2007.
13. *Indian Express*, September 12, 2008, p. 8.

6

Globalisation and Socio-economic Transformation: Boon or Bane

Introduction

Globalisation refers to increasing global connectivity, integration and interdependence in the economic, social, technological, cultural, political and ecological spheres. Globalisation is understood as rapid increase in cross-border economic, social and technological exchange and as a process leading to greater interdependence and mutual awareness among economic, political and social units in the world. It is taken as the emergence of altered global structures and driven by a skill revolution, an organisational explosion and a continuous flow of ideas, money, goods and reaching people hitherto restricted by human-made cultural and national boundaries. It offers a splendid opportunity for sharing products hitherto not reached by a section of world population as we have a global market. The supporters of globalisation always try to convince the world that it will create a new economic and social order where many of the boundaries will be broken to make the world a good place to live in.

Nobel laureate Joseph Stiglitz defined globalisation as removal of barriers to free trade and the closer integration of national economies.[1] In other words, economic globalisation refers to the integration of different economies of the world through trade, investments and migration of the people. Rangarajan understood globalisation as "integration of economies and societies through cross country flow of information, ideas, technology, goods, services, capital, finance and people."[2] This chapter evaluates the role of globalisation in the process of social transformation. The chapter tries to study, how globalisation has helped in socio-economic progress of developing countries in general and India in particular.

Demystification of Globalisation

In the early 1990, globalisation was welcomed with euphoria. Capital flows to developing countries had increased six fold in six years from 1990 to 1996. The establishment of the World Trade Organisation in 1995 was to bring the semblance of a rule of law to international commerce. Everyone was supposed to be the winner– those in both the developed and the developing world. Globalisation was to bring unprecedented prosperity to all.[3] The most popular conception of globalisation is the modern metaphor of a "global village." The metaphor is inspired from our ever-shrinking world in which we need to establish a community of international cooperation. A "global village" serves as a nice metaphor, but is very difficult to translate into reality. The form of globalisation that appears to be taking place is simply the evolution of a time-proven process. Globalisation is merely an outgrowth of trade between nations. Ever since the dawn of civilisation, individuals have realised the economic gains to be made through trade.

Basic economics indicates that two different individuals, communities, or nations have a comparative advantage in certain goods they produce. Trade then allows these individuals to produce certain goods and services to exchange with others. This results in an increased product from the division of labour and specialisation in production. While tangible items are the medium of trade, it is the exchange of intangible ideas that the process of free trade helps to foster. The Action Institute defines globalisation as: "A policy of free trade and economic engagement requires government to relinquish some of its power to the people and creates pockets of independent wealth that frees people from dependence upon the State for their material well being. Through trade important cultural and economic ties are also built between persons living within a country and with persons living abroad."[4]

The process of globalisation occurs through millions of decisions made by millions of individuals every day. No state directs these individuals as to what their interests should be. Each individual realises what goods, services, and ideas will satisfy their wants. Indeed, if the state did direct the decisions of these individuals it may very well lead down The Road to Serfdom, as described by Hayek. Adam Smith wrote in his famous work, The Wealth of Nations, "Every individual, it is evident, can, in his local situation judge much better than any statesman or lawgiver can do for him."[5]

Globalisation and Developing Nations

The advantages of globalisation to developing nations are clearly visible, but what will happen to the established communities of the developed world, and mainly the Western world is the matter of concern. Change may occur through Globalisation, however, the cross-cultural exchange of ideas is not to be feared, for our own society is formed from the cross mingling of many traditions. The Western tradition has formed from the Greeks, Romans, Hebrews and the English. Indian culture is a mix of culture and traditions that has formed over thousands of years, and survived the crises of the ages; it is unlikely to disappear in the near future. One can truly value the moral traditions that define our society, not only will they survive, but we can export them to other nations via the market of ideas. This may be the hidden beauty in an age of globalisation.

Every community may submit their traditions and morals for view in the international market. If we believe our traditions and values to be of importance, then we should feel comfortable in sharing them with others. The surest way to share a set of morals, character, or virtue is through persuasion. An English Scholar John Locke wrote: "The care of souls cannot belong to the civil magistrate, because his power consists only in outward force: but true and saving religion consists in the inward persuasion of the mind."[6]

Essentially, the ideas that individuals deem worth preserving will be separated from the chaff. Furthermore, every tradable good or service that leaves the shores of a nation serves as a bearer of peace. The lands that develop the best methods in education, the greatest degree of technology, and the most beautiful masterpieces of art are sure to impress the international community. The qualities of the goods that a nation develops serve as testimony to the excellence of the citizens within. Globalisation makes possible for every good trader to be a messenger of freedom, character, and effective government. Globalisation gives incentive for the cooperation between nations and individuals. A French scholar Alex de Tocqueville made his observation: "Trade is the natural enemy of all violent passions. Trade loves moderation, delights in compromise, and is most careful to avoid anger. It is patient, supple, and insinuating, only resorting to extreme means in cases of absolute necessity. Trade makes men independent of one another... it leads them to want to manage their own affairs and teaches them how to succeed therein. Hence it makes them inclined to liberty but disinclined to revolution."[7]

Many consider Globalisation incompatible with virtue, however; if we can promote the ideas of virtue to others through free exchange, then virtuousness will flourish. An English Economist, Adam Smith wrote: "Virtue is not said to amiable, or meritorious, because it is the object of its own love, or of its own gratitude; but because it excites those sentiments in other men."[8]

Globalisation in itself fosters worldwide the virtues of prudence, temperance and individualism. Individuals exercise good judgment in order to avoid disturbing the personal gains made possible through cooperative exchange. The politics and ideologies of radicalism cannot survive in a world of self-interest because extremism is a detriment to the well being of the individual. Milton Friedman wrote, "Self-interest is not myopic selfishness. It is whatever it is that interests the participants, whatever they value, whatever goals they pursue."[9]

Globalisation and Economic Prosperity

The economic prosperity that results from globalisation provides for political liberty. Political and economic liberty goes side by side. Globalisation allows for the economic dispersion of funds to the many, not through coercion or redistribution, but by the freedom to make one's own economic decisions. When the government holds less of the people's money, it returns to the original functions intended of government; protection of life, liberty, and property. When a government steps outside these bounds it typically encroaches upon individual liberty, thus trampling political liberty. With political liberty and the absence of the overbearing state, comes the power to direct one's community towards a beneficial character. When the role of government is limited, institutions such as the church, charity, and family flourish in local settings. With the absence of a benevolent welfare system, charitable care must be the bedrock of each community. Local citizens rely on each other and their institutions, rather than others many miles away.

This also gives strong compulsion for personal responsibility in looking after one's own survival. It is much harder to be a beggar in one's neighborhood, than to live off the fruits of a stranger. In other words, it is less likely one will depend on living off the labours of those he knows personally. Historically, character has best been administered in a local setting. Man grows in virtue through family, field, and the church. Since Globalisation results in creation of wealth, the community becomes the focal point, because large government is no longer needed to provide sustenance. It is presumed that Globalisation is a process that occurs through free trade. Adam Smith, the father of modern economics, wrote of an "invisible hand" that directs the market at all times. The character that exists in community is also directed by such an "invisible hand".

There has been the impact of globalisation on higher education. Despite gains in efficiency and productivity due to a better division of labour, it is often argued that in some respects globalisation works against the interest of developing countries, reinforcing international inequalities. The impact of globalisation is seen as being widespread. While there are concerns about integrating higher education into the legal structure of world trade through the WTO, cross-border activities in higher education are on the increase. Many countries are looking at the opportunities available and the risks associated with increased trade in higher education. All keep track of position and development taking place on higher education services by other countries in the GATS negotiations.

Globalisation and Social Transformation

Globalisation presents the largest new uncertainty in the realm of food security in India and other developing countries. The greatest hope of many leaders in India and in other developing countries is the promise of globalisation. Institutions such as GATT and the WTO no doubt reduces trade barriers, with the expectation that it will speed economic growth and bring industry, employment, and revenue from goods exports to developed countries. The cities will be filled with a new urban middle class, technology will flow freely from developed countries to developing ones, and the revenue earned from the huge amounts of exports can be used to uplift the poor, both urban and rural. Give it ten, twenty years of free trade and development, and the country will be a Utopian capitalist paradise of happy, well-fed, middle-class Indians with houses and cars and each their own TV. One of the greatest problems brought about by globalisation so far is that of decreased domestic food availability.

In India, exports of luxury agricultural crops have increased, while productivity and domestic food production have fallen. Proponents of globalisation would likely respond to this by asserting that it is merely a short-term problem. The promise of increased trade and fast economic growth should, in their minds, lead to a general improvement of economic conditions for the poor and an eventual end to poverty in the country. However, economic growth does not automatically mean a reduction in poverty. Though it can be a powerful tool to achieve such a goal, but does not necessarily bring about an upliftment of the poor.

Globalisation and Indian Economic Scenario

From 1950 to 1975, when economic growth averaged a healthy 3.6 per cent, poverty remained at generally stable levels. From 1975 to 1985, when poverty reduction was significant, the economy did grow at a faster 4 per cent; however, much of the reduction of poverty is attributable to increased agricultural production (agriculture being the most significant industry in India). In the late 1980s and early 1990s, when economic growth was even more rapid, poverty rates were generally flat and even increased when agricultural production fell due to adverse weather conditions in the early 1990's. Economic growth from 1950 to 1975 concentrated mostly on the enhancement of large-scale industry.

While this has the power to uplift lower-middle-class urban residents, it did not have an appreciable effect on the bulk of India's economic difficulty—the problem of the massive numbers of rural poor. Most Indians are employed in very small scale micro enterprises, not in factories. Health and educational services were built, but mostly in urban areas, thus inadequately serving the huge rural population. Agricultural growth was prompted by the Green Revolution, but not distributed very well throughout the country. Land reforms were introduced to favour small farmers over inefficient absentee landlords of large plots, but enforcement was very spotty. Central planning focused on large goals but the details failed to be fleshed out. The decreases in poverty accomplished in the late seventies and early eighties were mostly due to a few important factors: improvements in infrastructure, enforcement of land reforms, and the public food distribution system, which provides grain at fair prices to the country's poor. The Green Revolution's accelerated pace also played an important role in this improvement; however, the uneven distribution of the benefits of the Green Revolution leads to improvements only in certain areas. Great geographic disparities of economic well-being were accentuated by the Green Revolution.

Many of the land reforms and agricultural subsidies instituted to uplift India's rural poor are being challenged by globalisation. Land reforms instituted in the 1970's to address the problem of rural landless families and absentee landlords have been a crucial part of the advancement of the country's poor. But current trends advocate huge, mechanised farms, which are not possible under many of India's land holding ceilings. It is often claimed that large farms are very efficient, but that is mostly untrue. The "inefficient small farmer" is mostly a myth-while a large mechanised farm can produce more of any single product than a small farm, overall productivity is much lower. In India, farms smaller than 5 acres have productivity rates of some 735 Rupees (Rs.) per acre, while larger farms of 35 acres or more have productivity rates of a mere Rs.346 per acre. This is because most mechanised farms are a monoculture that focuses on production of one part of the plant, while small farms focus on diverse crops and on utilising every portion of the plant. In the state of Bengal, strong and effective land reforms divided many large farms into small farms, which gave it a 6.5 per cent growth rate, compared to the 3 per cent national average. And while small-scale agriculture may be much more labour-intensive, this is not a bad thing in a country of one billion inhabitants suffering from massive underemployment.

Given some of the negative effects experienced so far with globalisation and trade liberalisation, it is easy to wonder why the Indian government (as well as the governments of many other developing countries) would be pursuing it so enthusiastically. Certainly, the great promise of such successful economies as found in developed countries can be a powerful lure.

And economic growth can indeed be a powerful tool for socio-economic advancement. But intelligent, village-scale planning is essential to such improvement and current global trade policies focusing on the large-scale matter of gross "economic growth" and encouraging the liberalisation of markets is contrary to the needs of the people. Removal of public subsidies and repeal of land reforms encouraged by global trade policies will only further damage India's economic well-being. Massive multinational corporations pay farmers very low prices for goods then sell them at huge profits abroad, taking advantage of their dominance in the system and sucking massive amounts of capital and food from the country. India needs to develop its rural areas, encourage intensive small-scale community agriculture, and manage to feed all its people-all aims that are not aided by the current west-favouring global trade policies.

Globalisation and Agriculture Imbalances

Globalisation does not have any positive impact on agriculture. On the contrary it has little detrimental effect as government is always willing to import food grains, sugar etc whenever there is a price increase of these commodities. Government never thinks to pay more to farmers so that they produce more food grains but resorts to imports. On the other hand, subsidies are declining and the cost of production is increasing. Even forms producing fertilisers have to suffer due to imports. The ongoing process of globalisation has influenced all the sectors of economy including the agriculture sector. Globalisation has offered enormous opportunities but also threats to communities that are not adequately prepared to face its challenges. It has created turbulence, uncertainty, competitiveness, need for adaptation to change and timely adoption and absorption of technologies. "As the world is globalising, a global knowledge and information society is emerging, spanning all regions. Knowledge and information have become significant factors for production of goods and services. They affect the international division of labour, determine the competitiveness of economics and corporations, generate new growth patterns and in the process spawn new products, jobs and livelihoods"[10]

Poverty Alleviation and Bearing the Brunt of Globalisation

The globalisation has affected the poor and illiterate people of the world particularly the rural people and small farmers having small land holdings. Moreover many of them have no access to information and other facilities that can help to enhance their participation in economic development, improve their productivity, income and living conditions. "Of the world $1.09 billion extremely poor people, about 74 percent (810 million) live in marginal areas and rely on small scale agriculture for their livelihood. In most developing countries, agriculture continues to be the most important sector of the economy, accounting for the biggest proportion of employment"[11] The irony of the situation is that many of the small farmers engaged in agriculture are undernourished. They are producers but not the consumers of food because of poverty. "In the overall, the number of hungry people in the developing world has increased by 34 million from mid I990s to stand at 8I5 million in 2002."[12] This number has increased further as the benefits of development are not reaching the masses in the developing countries. "Most of the 842 undernourished people in the developing world today are from farming families in developing countries."[13] Lack of rural infrastructure and low income let the things go on as they are going on and acts as impediments to speed up the process of rural development. "In 2003, close to 700 million Asians were estimated to be living on less than a dollar a day"[14] In spite of improvements in agricultural production, the poverty alleviation programmes are not making a substantial headway in many developing countries. For instance in India, the drought conditions at some places and floods and hailstorms at other places cause loss of crops. Due to globalisation there is a real threat for decline in prices of agriculture products. On the other hand a constant increase in crop inputs is also causing a concern for farmers and several small farmers have started thinking that agriculture is not a viable occupation.

There are other global changes that are hitting the small farmers and threatening food security of nations. "A recent study shows how temperature changes are already hitting the global economy with the Indian agriculture bearing its brunt. The study proves that agriculture losses worth $5 billion annually, from 1981-2002, can be correlated with temperature rises over that period. The study appearing in Environmental Research Letters, a reputed journal published from the UK has shown that almost 30 per cent variation in the global agriculture yields can be explained by temperature rise. With wheat, barley and maize being the three crops hit the maximum due to temperature rise, India, the second largest producer of wheat and the fifth largest producer of maize in the world, is obviously suffering silent kill on its agrarian economy".[15]

With the increasing use of chemical fertilizers, the soil salinity is increasing and soil conditions do not help to enhance agriculture production. On one hand there are challenges to feed the growing number of the Indian population and on the other hand several problems are cropping in the way of increasing the agricultural production. The future increase of agricultural production will be realised through integrated knowledge applications such as greater use of biotechnology, more effective irrigation management and soil preparation, avoiding environmental degradation and cutting costs wherever possible.

The poverty reduction and national development effort in the developing countries cannot succeed without improving the economic conditions and effective participation of rural populations, majority of which constitute small farmers. Timely accessibility to appropriate information and eradication of illiteracy from rural areas can help in alleviation of rural poverty. The United Nations has addressed the issue of illiteracy in its eight Millennium Development Goals (MDGs) for poverty reduction by addressing the goal of universal primary education. One of the goals of the United Nations in MDGs is to ensure environmental sustainability. Developing Countries and poor nations should make efforts to preserve environment through the use of environment friendly technologies and farming practices. "Organic agriculture is likely to benefit the poor living in marginal areas the most, by improving productivity and incomes, and providing environmental sustainability. In Thailand, contract organic rice farming in marginal areas has produced significant livelihood improvements for participating farmers."[16]

Organic farming is finding favour in resource poor areas. There are now abundant choices and farming technologies in knowledge intensive agriculture work and most appropriate decision making pertaining to what is relevant for which area is thus very crucial for agricultural growth and development. Abundance of knowledge in the field of agriculture has accumulated out of the outcomes and experiences of various farming practices in various parts of the world. "For instance, farmers in Southern Sudan and Zaire noticed that the sites of termite moulds are particularly good for growing sorghum and cowpea. Farmers in Zaachilla, Mexico use ant refuse to fertilise high value crops such as tomatoes, chili and onions."[17] Some of the accumulated knowledge of years remained confined to communities and not even documented, and thus remained inaccessible to other farming communities.

Globalisation and Exchange of Information

Globalisation and rapid exchange of information made possible by developments in information technologies have facilitated global access to local knowledge and vice-versa. As far as agricultural development is concerned India is a unique country among the developing world. The most advanced as well as the most primitive kind of agricultural technologies are practiced in the country. On one hand there are most modern agricultural implements such as tractors and harvesting combines, on the other hand there are millions of farmers using bullock carts and ploughs. There are areas like Chirapunji where it rains all the time and there are places in Rajasthan which often witness drought conditions. Diversity of soil and climatic conditions are existing in the country and hence India is known for its diversity of plant species and varieties of crops. Even system of medicine namely Ayurveda is based mainly on formulations made from various medicinal plants. The country has diverse geographical settings such as hilly terrains, wet lands, valleys, deserts and sea coast.

A variety of crops can thus be grown and various agricultural technologies can be adopted and adapted to specific needs. There are farmers who have developed hundreds of web pages of agriculture information and communicate through email and there are also the farmers who still dispatch their messages. There are hundreds of languages spoken and several ethnic groups of farmers living in various cultural settings and having different belief and ethical systems. The major problems of Indian agriculture are fragmented farms, monsoon dependent irrigation in several areas, disrupted power-supply, increasing cost of farm inputs, non-availability of international quality seeds, exploitation of poor and illiterate farmers by intermediaries and lending institutions, lack of adequate information pertaining to what can be most useful and relevant in a given area and situation. Small farm holdings are one of the barriers to modernisation and automation of agricultural farms. There is an enormous fluctuation in the prices of agricultural commodities. The prices of onions or tomato may be Rs. 2/- when the farmers sell it but may increase ten times up to Rs. 20/- when sold in the retail market at a different time and such price hikes not only affect the farmers but severely affect the pocket of common man and polity of the nation. The increasing cost of agricultural inputs and comparatively low cost of agricultural products in the international market is creating a crisis situation for Indian agriculture. For instance it is cheaper to buy wheat from the international market than buy it from the Indian market and some mill owners prefer to import instead of buying it locally. Similarly it is cheaper to buy milk and milk products from the international markets than buying it from the Indian markets. The constantly growing input cost of agriculture is affecting the small farmers and their families. The small farmers are increasingly under debt and under stress. According to a recent study[18] conducted by the Punjab Agricultural University, Ludhiana around 89 per cent of the farmers in the State of Punjab is under debt. "In India 70 per cent of farmers are cultivators of small plots from which they can hardly get food security let alone sustainable incomes."

Most of them are small and marginal farmers cultivating land less than one hectare in size, average size of which decreases by half every 15 years due to rapid population growth. "Today nearly 60 per cent of farmers belong to marginal category with an average of 0.4 ha. Land."[19]. Small land holdings, growing cost of production, increasing debt, low prices of some agricultural commodities in the international markets is aggravating the problems of small farmers and leading to some suicides. Hundreds of farmers in the Vidarbha region have committed suicides and such incidences have also been reported from other parts of India. The National Knowledge Commission (NKC) set up by the Government of India in its report to the nation 2006 recorded. "Agriculture provides the principal means of livelihood for over 60 per cent of India's population. Despite a steady decline in its share of the Gross Domestic Product (GDP) it remains the largest economic sector in the country. Low and volatile growth rates and the recent escalation of an agrarian crisis in several parts of the Indian country side are a threat not only to national food security, but also to the economic well being of the nation as a whole."[20]

The National Knowledge Commission report of 2006 has identified several areas of intervention within agriculture, examining the traditional agricultural practices, held meeting in conjunction with the Indian Council of Agricultural Research (ICAR) focusing areas like post harvest infrastructure, organic farming, integrated pest management programmes and energy management in agriculture. "The National Knowledge Commission has begun work on agriculture research and extension systems to enhance and expand mechanisms for the creation and dissemination of relevant social and scientific knowledge". The globalisation has also offered immense opportunities for Indian farmers to export their agriculture products in world markets, concentrate on herbs and agricultural commodities that are in great demand in world markets, e.g., Indian mangoes, and other fruits. The globalisation has brought greater awareness of opportunities and alternatives for farmers to enhance their incomes from farming. "By switching from subsistence farming to cash crop farming Maharashtra small farmers have gained an additional $200 - $400 in income per year".[21]

The globalisation is helping to bridge the technological gap and provide solutions to problems with the help of developed countries and international organisations. It is often quoted to indicate the technological gap that it requires three times the effort to produce a ton of rice in India than in the United States. "Now a major agricultural transformation developed with the help of USAID is sweeping across India's northern rice and wheat growing belt and helping farmers save time as well as preserve precious natural resources." "Globalisation in the context of agriculture can best be discussed in the context of three components improvement of productive efficiency by ensuring the convergence of potential and realised outputs, increase in agricultural exports and value added activities using agricultural produce, and finally improved access to domestic and international markets that are either tightly regulated or overly protected".[22]

Globalisation however is likely to have a profound influence on food processing cottage industries and big industrial houses are likely to venture in the area of food processing for greater profitability through exports of such products that are in demand in international markets e.g., mango pulp. Globalisation is also influencing the marketing of fresh agriculture produce. The component of population is determining the imperatives and dynamics of new business environment in India. "Fresh produce retailing through supermarkets, with integrated supply chains back to the farm is growing rapidly in India. From close to zero in the recent past this market segment is expected to make up over a third of the market in the next several years! This is a stunning development and calls for radical changes in existing marketing relationships. This is significant because marketing is often neglected by farmers especially small farmers—yet it is vital to their income."[23]

The globalisation has helped in the mobility of foreign flowers in India and Indian mangoes abroad. The developments in ICT too have facilitated to the global agriculture knowledge. What is lacking is strategy and agility on the part of government machinery to put the existing infrastructure to best possible use, identify gaps and quickly attend to the problem areas. The private sector steps in where the public sector keeps thinking only. The success story of ITCs e-choupals in rural India indicates that a lot of potential for development exists in rural India. The development process will hasten if agricultural development and small farmers development go hand in hand. There is a need to constantly build and improve rural infrastructure such as improving irrigation, electric supply and building a type of public libraries that may act as local gateways to global knowledge. Such public libraries will not only provide access to desired knowledge but also keep the rural youth away from many social evils, help them to realise their true potentialities and keep them aware of opportunities that are existing for them. Rural development in India should be a mission accomplished through synergy of man\ongoing efforts and coordination of various activities like transfer of knowledge and information for various developmental activities should he an important component. There is an urgent need for imparting information literacy to farmers and build their capacities so that they can competently face new developments in agriculture. There is also need for cross disciplinary communication of information from related areas such as ethno-botany. Biotechnology, environmental sciences for sustainable agriculture development so that agricultural productivity can be increased, and farmers' economic position improved without degradation of planet earth. Mahatma Gandhi said that earth provides enough to satisfy everyman's need, but not every man's greed.

Conclusion

The globalisation has somehow helped the developing nations towards their national economy. In the field of agriculture, globalisation has brought revolution for the rural mass has to get profit of it or bear the brunt of globalisation. No doubt in the field of information and technology, it has helped the small farmers or marginalised farmers. With the modern technology and information concerning to seeds and fertiliser, the output has been realised. It has not only made an impact on Indian economy, but it has affected positively on Indian education system. It has opened new avenues for Indian as well as foreign students' 'exchange program and exchange of ideas.' It can be viewed as boon as well as bane for developing nation.

Endnotes

1. Stiglitz, Joseph. (2002). Globalisation and Its Discontents, England: Penguin, p. ix.
2. Rangarajan C. (2003), "Globalisation and its Impact" in Uma Kapila, "Indian Economy Since Independence" New Delhi: Academic Foundation. p. 729.
3. Joseph Stiglitz (2006), Making Globalisation Work, Penguin: Allen Lane, p. 7.
4. "Globalisation" Acton institute, 01 December 2006, <http://www.acton.org/ppolocy/trade/globe>.
5. Smith,Adam. "Free Trade" The Libertarian Reader, Ed. David Boaz. New York. The Free Press, 1997, p. 261.
6. Locke, John. "Understanding can not be compelled." The Libertarian Reader Ed. David Boaz, New York, Free Press. 1997, p. 53.

7. Tocqueville, Alesis De. Democracy in America, Yew York. Perennial Classic, 2000, p. 637.
8. Polachek, Solomon W. and Seiglie, Carlos, "Trade, Peace and Democracy: An Analysis of Dyadic Disputes" (June 2006) Institute for the Study of Labour Discussion Paper No. 2170, http//ssrn.com/abstract=915360.
9. Smith, Adam. "Justice and Beneficence." The Libertarian Reader. Ed David Boaz New York: Free Press, 1997, p. 60.
10. Asian Technology Parks: Lessons for the "Digital Divide" (Proposal to TheFordFoundationAugust2000) Available :http://www2.eastwestcenter.org/research/itparks/proposal.htm.|
11. Bage, Lennart (2005) Statement delivered on the Launch of the MDG Report - 18, January 2005. Available:http://www.ifad.org/events/mdg/ifad.htm.
12. Prolinnova. http://www.oaklandinstitute.org/?q=node/view/159).
13. *Ibid.*
14. Setboonsarng, Sununtar (2006) Organic Agriculture. Poverty Reduction and the Millennium Development Goals. (Paper presented at International Workshop on Sufficiency Economy, Poverty Reduction, and the MDGs Organised under the umbrella of the Exposition of Sufficiency Economy for Sustainable Development). Available: http://www.adbi.org/files/ 2006.09.
15. Sethi, Nitin (2007) $5 billion worth crops destroyed annually. The Times of India (New Delhi) Wednesday, April 4. 2007.
16. Setboonsarng, Sununtar. (2006), op. cit.
17. Reijntjes, C. and B. Haverkort and A. Waters-Bayer (1992) Farming for the future: An introduction tolow-external input and sustainable agriculture. London: Macmillan.Aval lable:http://www.ciesin.columbia.edu/docs/004-176a/permit.htm.
18. Devinder Pal and Satrajit Chakarbarti (2007) 89 pc of farmers under debt. *The Tribune* 1 27(9?), April 7, 2007.
19. IDEI (International Development Enterprises. India. Natural Resource conservation. Available: http://www.ide-india.org/ide/socialimpact.shtml.
20. Government of India, National Knowledge Commission. Report to the Nation, p. 22.

21. USAID (US Agency for International Development). Technology Broadens Farmers Markets. Available: http://www.usaid.gov/in/Pdfs/Farmer_Markets.pdf.

22. Vlahadevan, Renuka (2003) Productivity Growth in Indian Agriculture: The Role of Globali/alion and Economic Reform. Asia Pacific Development Journal 10(2), p. 59.

23. Deikun, George (2007) Remarks by George Deikun, USAID India Mission Director, at the Opening of the "Linking Markets and Farmers" Conference, New Delhi.

7

Problems of Rural Consumers in India: An Analysis

Introduction

There are about 6, 38, 365 villages in India. Around 70 per cent of our consumers' populations live in rural area. In our country a substantial number of rural people are living below the poverty line having high level of unemployment and poor literacy level. As they are illiterate, they are easily cheated by traders. Rural consumers are exploited due to ignorance and lack of unity among them. They are exploited in the rural market on account of lack of competition among sellers since there are only one or two petty shops available in rural places and the consumers have no choice. The main problem faced by rural consumers is related to adulteration, short weight and measures, fake brands and spurious products and misleading advertisements and imitation. They are facing hardship in reaching semi-urban places for getting good products and better services for want of money and time at their disposal.

Consumer is one who consumes certain goods and avails of certain services for which she/he pays, is a consumer. At the same time a person who buys goods or avails of services exclusively for the purpose of earning his/her livelihood by means of self-employment, comes under the definition of consumer. In order to protect the consumers, Government has taken a significant step by amending the

Consumer Protection Act 1986. The new provision incorporated the Mahatma Gandhi's perception that "Consumer is the King," in this Act. This Act extends to the whole of India except the state of Jammu and Kashmir. According to Section 2(1) (d) of 1986 Act, Consumer means any person who buys any goods or hires or avails of any services for a consideration which has been paid or promised or partly paid or partly promised or under any system of different payment, but does not include a person who obtains such goods for resale or for any commercial purpose. In this chapter an effort is made to understand the problems of rural consumers and try to find out solutions. Before one study the problem of rural consumer it would pertinent to know the Consumer Protection Act, 1986.

Consumer Protection Act, 1986

Consumer is one of the important components of the economy. He is one of the participants in the process of production. He performs an important role on both the sides 'demand' and 'supply'. A consumer is considered to be an important entity in market oriented economy. The attractive advertisement, packaging and salesmanship influence the consumer's demand. Many times consumers, especially in rural areas, are cheated, and therefore, need some sort of legal protection. For this purpose a number of Acts have been passed and the Consumers' Protection Act is the most important one among them. The Consumer Protection Act 1986 was enacted with the object to the interest of consumers at large.

Purpose of the Consumer Protection, Act:

The main purpose of passing the Consumers' Protection Act is clearly maintained in the preamble of the Act, which states:

1. The Act is basically passed to protect the interests of the consumers.
2. The Act makes provisions for setting up of a machinery to settle consumers' grievances.
3. The Act intends to seek speedy and simple redressal to consumer disputes through quasi-judicial machinery set up at the District, State and Central levels.

These quasi-judicial bodies are expected to observe the principles of natural justice. They have been empowered to give relief of a specific nature and to award compensation to aggrieved consumers on the basis of merit of each case.

The Act defines the consumer as any person who buys any commodity or service or a user of such commodity or service. However, if an individual buys a commodity for the purpose of resale or trading will not be treated as a 'consumer'. The spirit of the Act is to provide protection to persons who really use and consume the goods and services. Any person claiming himself as consumer must satisfy two conditions:

(i) The service must have been rendered to him, and

(ii) He must have paid or promised to pay for the same.

If a person buys a car, *autorikshaw* or a Xerox machine for earning his livelihood and finds any defect in it, he can approach the consumer grievances redressal machinery. The Act recognises such persons as consumers. The Act provides variety of rights to consumers.

Rights of the Consumers

Consumers' Protection Act, 1986 recognises the following rights of consumers.

1. ***Right to safety:*** Every consumer has a right to be safeguarded and protected from goods which are dangerous or harmful to life and property, e.g., colours used in food products, toys, home appliances, etc.
2. ***Right to information:*** The consumers have the right to be informed about the quality, quantity, potency, purity, standard and the price while choosing a commodity or service for purchase.
3. ***Right to choose:*** The consumers have the right to be assured, wherever possible, an access to a variety of goods at competitive prices. This right will help the consumers to make a choice of selecting goods and services according to their financial ability and preferences.

4. ***Right to be heard:*** Consumers have the right to express their opinions regarding the quality and prices of the commodities or services. Their views should receive due consideration from manufacturers, sellers and traders. Many business houses have their Consumer Affairs Departments to entertain the consumer's feedback about their products and services.
5. ***Right to seek redressal:*** Every consumer has the right to seek redressal of grievances before the Consumers' Redressal Agencies, namely, the District Forum, the State Commission and the National Commission.
6. ***Right to environment:*** Consumer has the right to enjoy clean and pollution free environment. If any factory or business unit creates pollution by means of garbage, air, water or sound in the locality, the consumer can lodge a complaint in writing and claim redressal.
7. ***Right to consumer education:*** Every consumer has the right to receive information about low quality, spurious, adulterated and dangerous goods through posters, exhibitions and literature, etc., through whatever other media.

Promotion of Consumer Education by Government

The slogan '*Jago Grahak Jago*' has now become a household name as a result of the publicity campaign undertaken in the last 5 years. It can be seen almost every day in the news papers. It has been making people aware their rights and tells them that before one buys any goods one must see the expiry dates. Through the increased thrust on consumer awareness in the 11th Five Year Plan, the Government has endeavoured to inform the common man of his rights as a consumer. As part of the consumer awareness scheme, the rural and remote areas have been given top priority.

A full-fledged Department of Consumer Affairs has been created, which tries to provide consumer education through seminars in different educational institutions. Special programmes have also been telecasted on *Lok Sabha TV and Doordarshan* to highlight the issues relating to consumer awareness. Issues pertaining to rural and remote areas have been given prominence in the various advertisement spots.

Consumer awareness messages are also being disseminated through Meghdoot Postcards in consultation with Department of Post to reach far-flung rural areas including North-East States. Posters carrying messages pertaining to consumer awareness have been displayed in 1.55 lakh Rural Post Offices and more than 25000 Urban Post Offices throughout the country.

The Department has launched a *National Consumer Help Line.* The toll free number 1800-11-4000 facility is available to consumers from 9.30 am to 5.30 pm on all the working days. The Department has launched on March 15, 2005 Consumer on Line Resources and Empowerment (CORE) Centre on the website www.core.nic.in for consumer advocacy and online redressal of consumer grievances. Through the various advertisements relating to consumer awareness, adequate publicity is being given to the activities of CORE and its website so that consumers can take the help of online counseling/guidance being provided through it. The Department has initiated a policy of setting up a *National Consumer Protection Authority,* which would be a proactive body empowered to take *suo moto* action for better protection of the interests of the consumers in general. This Department is also in the process of framing a 'National Consumer Policy' which would shape the future of consumer movement in the country. Under this policy, it is proposed to attune the consumer movement in the country with the United Nations Guidelines on Consumer Protection. Through news papers the department of Consumer Affairs has been trying to education the Indian mass. The day is therefore not far off when the consumers will be truly empowered.

Absence of Redressal Mechanism in Rural Areas

When the rural market grows in such a rapid pace, the quantum of consumer grievances also increases simultaneously. The main problems faced by rural consumers are related to adulteration, short weighing and measuring, lack of safety and quality in appliances and equipment, unfair warranties and guarantees, unreasonable pricing etc. The Indian Consumer Protection Act 1986 ensure better protection of rights and interest of people who are consumers in one way or the other from the exploitation of trade and industries. According to the Act, anyone who buys goods and services for his/her use is a consumer. A user of such goods and services with the permission of the buyer is also a consumer. The Department of Consumer Affairs of the Government of India and various state governments has undertaken a number of innovative measures to protect rights of rural consumers. Consumer disputes redressal mechanism (popularly known as consumer forums) are set up under the Act at district, state and national level to provide simple and inexpensive quick redressal against consumer complaints. A consumer can file complaint in the consumer court against any defective goods purchased or deficient service rendered including restrictive/unfair trade practice adopted by any trader/person. The Consumer Forum has power to order removal/replacement of defects/deficiencies in goods and services, refund of price paid, compensation for loss/injury suffered, discontinuation of unfair/restrictive trade practice, withdrawal of hazardous or unsafe goods or award of adequate cost to the parties etc. Despite the fact that out of 644 District Consumer forums, 616 are not functioning properly. There are over 3.7 lakh cases are pending in various consumer courts.

Total number of consumer complaints filed and disposed Since inception of the Consumer Protection Act 1986

Name of Agency	*Cases filed since inception inception*	*Cases disposed of since inception*	*Cases pending*	*% of total disposal*
National Commission	92,481	81,039	11,442	87.63%
State Commission	6, 61, 295	5,70, 184	91,111	86.22%
District Commission	34,82,728	32,13,497	2,69,231	92.27%
Total	**42, 36, 504**	**38, 64, 720**	**3,71, 784**	**91.22%**

Source: Ministry of Consumer Affairs, Food and Public Distribution, 2013.

However, the three-tier consumer forums, set up under the Act are in urban areas. These data is from three-tier situated in Cities/ town/States. It difficult for rural consumers to approach the forum. Moreover, though the forum have been set up as special courts, the non-extension of their benches in rural areas makes accessibility a big problem and leading to poor public participation.

While experts and consumer activists believe that redressal platforms can forge consumer activism in rural areas, the government is undecided about setting up such a mechanism below the district level. The Department of Consumer Affairs has been organising consumer rights' awareness events in all *talukas*. As of now, there are no plans to extend the sittings of the *lok adalats* to villages or to set up redressal platforms there. The absence of laboratories at district level to test disputed products further makes the process delayed. In this context, the local administrative bodies should come forward and protect the rights of the rural consumers.

Rural consumers are fundamentally different from urban counterparts. The lower levels of literacy and limited exposure to products and services are well-known, but there are also differences in occupation options, with a direct impact on income levels and income flows and a high level of inter-dependency affecting the dynamics of rural community behaviour. All these contribute to the behaviour of rural consumers. There are several factors which contribute to influencing buying behaviour in rural India, like environment of the consumer, geographic influences, family economic factors, creative use of the products, etc.

The rural people, comprising of poor farmers, may not be much aware of the malpractices going on in the market due to their ignorance and high level of literacy. At the same time one finds that rural consumers are unorganised. This is due to the nature of the rural markets which covers a large area and less population density as per separate class and protect their consumer rights under both consumer law and competition law.

Factors Leading Consumer Exploitation

In India, rural consumers generally face a number of problems. They include non-availability of goods, adulteration, hoarding, black marketing, deceptive and misleading selling techniques and false warranties or guarantees, etc. There are number of factors which are responsible for the exploitation of rural consumers, viz., High Price,

Poor Quality of goods, Lack of Knowledge, Unorganised group of consumer, unorganised group of consumer, Unfair trade practices, Lack of coordination, Intangible services, Multiplicity of Weights and measures, Market oriented production. One can study these factors one by one.

1. **High Price:** Sometimes, artificial shortage of commodities is created in the market. Consumers are compelled to buy the commodities at high price. There may not be actually shortage of goods, but they are kept in the go-down so that it can be taken out when goods are completely exhausted. The villagers being ignorant about their consumer rights are exploited frequently.

2. **Poor quality of goods:** There is a general feeling that in India especially in rural area, the quality of goods or services has been declining. Manufacturers, in expectation of greater profit, increase production, but neglect the quality aspect of production. Many reputed firms have their own quality control departments, but the number of such firms is very limited. The quality of the products can be deteriorated due to adulterated material used in production. Such adulteration is very dangerous to health.

3. **Lack of Knowledge:** The Consumer Protection Act confers on the consumer the right to be informed about the quality, quantity, purity, standard and price of goods. Sometimes the goods demanded by the consumers are not available in the market. Consumers are compelled to purchase the unknown substitutes. Consumers do not get the full information about the quality of the product. They have to buy inferior goods at high prices due to lack of information. Because of their ignorance, rural mass fall prey of exploitation.

4. **Unorganised group of consumer:** The Producers are organised lot. They can determine the prices of their products. Hence, they sell their products at exorbitantly higher prices. The consumers on the other hand are" unorganised. He is not in a position to demand justice. They are misled and deceived by the manufacturers and traders while purchasing goods or hiring services. In the villages, people are busy with their cultivation and are not organised. Hence, they become the victim of exploitation. In order to get justice, they can think of *nyaya panchayat.*

5. **Misleading advertisements:** Advertisement is a powerful media of mass communication. Consumers get information about the arrival of new products in the market through different advertising media. Sometimes the consumers are misled by false advertisements. The manufacturers also use advertisement as a tool to create artificial demand for undesirable goods. Rural mass being ignorant are attracted by new items in the market. There is not expiry dates on the new goods nor have they branded name.

6. **Unfair trade practices:** Consumers face various problems due to unfair trade practices adopted by the producers. Unfair Trade Practice means a trade practice, which for the purpose of promoting the sale, use or supply of any goods or for the provision of any service, adopts any unfair or deceptive practice. For example one can see the false representation that the goods or services are of a particular standard, quality, quantity, grade, etc. Some time old goods are sold as new goods by changing the wrappers. Manufacturer gives to the public warranty and guarantee which sellers do not provide.

7 **Lack of coordination:** There is no coordination amongst the consumers, traders, manufacturers and the government. That means that there is no interaction between them due to which the interest of the consumer is not protected. In rural areas all are busy with their work. *Sarpach* has no time to listen to the grievances of consumers in the village. It is the *sarpach* and *gram sabha* should coordinate the consumers in the village.

8. **Intangible services:** The services offered by producers are intangible. A consumer has a right to see, touch, smell, hear or taste the product before purchasing. But it is not applicable to services. They are not able to touch the products. They are told, "If you want to take it, pay money otherwise go away." Thereby the consumers are cheated while purchasing the services.

9 **Multiplicity of Weights and measures:** The illiterate consumers are cheated due to multiplicity of weights and measures. They create uncertainty, especially in the rural marketing. Some time piece of brick or stone is used to measure the grains in rural areas. The measuring weight are not passed by the passing authority, hence

rural people depend on the old weight. Most of them are not aware that measuring weights are to be passed periodically.

10. **Market oriented production:** The production of goods is market oriented. The goods produced in the economy satisfy the wants of upper and middle classes. The production should cater to the needs of the people of lower classes. Some traders do not give proper treatment to poor customers. Because any production for poor does not provide enough profit. Therefore, their wants are ignored. Some farmers think of cultivating cash product like sugar cane, soybean etc. There is scanty eatable grain available for rural mass. And cash product are sold in towns.

Consumer Protection and Role of Local Bodies

Like in many other countries, consumer movement in India as a social force originated with the necessity of protecting and promoting the interest of consumers' against fraudulent, unethical and unfair trade practices. The movement initially reflected a common perception, which characterised traders and manufacturers as people who were out to maximise profits by means of fair or foul with scant regard for consumers' well-being. Selective shopping could be the only form of consumer resistance at the early stages, the basic tenet governing the legal position of consumers being 'buyers beware'. The movement gained a momentum after enactment of Consumer protection Act in 1986. Today it has 25 years of enactment of Consumer Protection Act. Over time the movement found expression in efforts to bring pressure on business firms as well as government to correct business conduct that may be unfair and against the interest of consumers at large. The movement, which has been confined to the middle class citizens in urban centres by large, is now having a presence in the rural areas as well. But it has to spread and strengthened further among the masses in rural and semi-urban areas.

The fact is that majority of consumers in the country are even unaware of the existence of consumer forums to which they can make their grievances. A CAG-commissioned survey finding on the status of the Consumer Protection Act (1986) conducted in 2006, says that 82 per cent of the consumers are not aware of the

Consumer Protection Act and 66 per cent of their rights. The ground reality is that the conditions are not very favourable and conducive for the consumer. Ignorance is one of the prominent factors contributing in the exploitation of the consumers and is most prevalent amongst the rural masses. The *Gram Panchayats* are there in all the villages, which is the available constitutional mechanism across the country spread in all 627 districts. It is only through this constitutional mechanism that the consumer movement can get a boost and consumer awareness can be spread among rural masses.

Consumer Awareness Campaign: A Solution

To meet the challenges, consumers must be made aware of Consumer Protection Act 1986. A consumer's best defence is knowledge of his/her rights as a consumer and of the remedies which exist to resolve these problems when they occur. The various stakeholders in the consumer protection movement need to work out a strategy to address the problems of the consumers. Creating awareness and educating the consumers will go a long way in helping the consumer to understand what constitutes consumer protection, what is the need to know about one's rights and how to redress one's grievances if anything goes wrong. Moreover, an educated and informed consumer will be able to take a rational decision while buying a product or availing a service.

The rural consumer has to be educated about resource maintenance and environment preservation. The rural consumers have to be educated about the possible exploitation of their resources and the subsequent detrimental changes in their life styles, if they are not protective of their environment and yield to the pressure that booming urban markets exert upon rural areas.

Consumer education should foster mutual awareness and understanding between the urban and rural sectors as well as rich and poor sections of society. Consumer education can strengthen the bonds that exist between various social segments and minimise the divisive factors. The market and the industry seek to widen the gaps that exist and seek to rule consumers through fostering divisions. The Consumer education programmes whether at *gram panchayat,* school and college levels or through government or NGO channels should seek to remove these distances.

Local self Government is the best forum to educate the rural masses about their rights as consumers as well as the techniques to redress their grievances, which are attended by almost every villager. On occasions like December 24, which is the National Consumer Day, meetings of the *Gram Sabha* need to be convened, where the villagers could properly be educated about their rights as consumers.

The *Local Self Government* could play a significant role in creating awareness at the grassroots level. Appropriate technology and creative media could be used to raise awareness. The relevant resource materials in regional languages could be made available in hard copies as well as in soft copies through internet. The *Local Self Government* can consider using media such as documentary films, street plays, competitions etc. to spread consumer awareness. The services of government primary school teachers could be utilised in conducting consumer awareness programmes. 'Complaints Box or Cell could be opened in each of the *Gram Panchayat* offices. This can act as an advice giving and complaints handling mechanism between the common consumer and the district consumer forum. This will help in speedy resolution of the complaints without taking it to the consumer forums as well as substantially reduce the burden of district forums.

Selected representatives from each of the *gram panchayats* can be identified and be trained to handle these cells. Issues at local level affecting the consumers can be discussed and disposed at this level only instead of taking each complaint to the district forum. Similar mechanism could be established at *Taluka* (Block) level as well. A selected group consisting of *Gram Sevak, Sarpanch*, school teachers, youth, can be trained for this purpose. Personal consumer advice could also be provided not only for legal problems, but also for every day consumer problems. Required budgetary allocations have to be made to *Gram Sabha* for consumer awareness. The *Local Self Government* can be a means for consumer education for the rural mass.

Suggestions and Conclusion

It is high time that the *Local Self Government* should come forward and take a lead in consumer education in their respective areas. Disadvantaged consumers are not able to assert their rights. Rural consumers remain disadvantaged as their right to information, choice, redress, and consumer education are not sufficiently fulfilled. Consequently such consumers need support in maintaining their rights so that they can bargain equally with the producers and the service providers. There are significant differences in the levels of awareness and literacy among the rural and urban consumers. Per capita income in rural area is half of that of urban areas. Value for money is more important to rural people. They buy small quantities and more frequently. The most common communication platforms in rural markets include *haats, melas, mandis* and other places of public gathering. While communicating with the rural masses it is required that the message delivered should be simple and direct to be effective. Local Self-Government can promote the right of rural consumer through different ways, putting poster on *Chawks,* sending SMS to member of *Gram Sabha* about the consumer awareness program, holding public meeting about consumer campaign program. It can put poster on the ration shop such as, *Jago Grahak Jago.* During the weekly *bazzar,* the *gram sabha* could distribute leaflets and show some documentary film on consumer awareness. In every *gram sabha* meeting the *sarpanch* should evaluate the cases of consumer exploitation. Through street play, the *gram sabha* can impart consumer education. It the villagers themselves can provide consumer education in their *panchayat.* It is the need of the hour.

References

1. Pradeep S. Mehta, 'How to Survive as a Consumer', CUTS, 1998, CUTS Publication.
2. Rama Bijapurkar and Rajesh Shukla 'Spotlight on rural consumers', December 3, 2008, Livemint.com.
3. Rama Bijapurkar and Rajesh Shukla 'The Rural Consumer Myth – II', March 26, 2009, Livemint.com

4. 'The 'Bird of Gold: The Rise of India's Consumer Market' May 2007, McKinsey and Company.

5. Chandwani, and Sanjay. 'Marketing To Rural Consumers', Vision, Apr-Jun 2009, Vol. 13, Issue-2.

6. Sanal Kumar Velayudhan, 'Rural Marketing: Targeting the Non-Urban Consumer', Response books, Sage Publications, Second Edition.

7. History of *Panchayati Raj* in India, available at:*http://en.wikipedia.org/wiki/History_of_panchayati_raj_in_India*

8. CUTS Report of *Upbhokta Mitra* Training (UMT) programme, 2000.

8

Judicial Activism: Bulwark of Indian Democracy

Genesis and Meaning of Judicial Activism

The concept of judicial activism is a recent origin and has given rise to many controversies. Some people consider this as a threat to the concept of separation of powers, which is considered sacred to our modern democracy. What is judicial activism? It is the willingness and inclination of judges to overturn legislation or executive action. When was the term Judicial Activism coined in Modern democracy? Theory of separation of power was popularised by Montesquieu. The traces of Judicial Activism can be found in the writings of Montesquieu, a French scholar, who wrote his famous work on 'The Spirit of the Laws' in 1748. Montesquieu wanted to separate the legislature, executive and judicial functions of the Government into three separate agencies.

In the United States of America it was Chief Justice John Marshall who delivered his historic judgment in case of Marbury vs. Madison and established the judicial supremacy. It was first used to protect the Constitution against any encroachment by the Executive or the Legislature. This became as a weapon to declare any executive order or legislative enactment as *ultra virus* if they do not go in consonance with the Constitution. No doubt it was opposed by both the branches of government, but was supported by the American people. Usually one ascribes to the origin of the doctrine of judicial review to Marbury vs. Madison case in the United States. If one takes the Indian context, the concept was realised way back in 1893. It was, Justice Syed Mahmood (1850-1903), Puisne Judge of the Allahabad high Court (1887-1893) (then North-Western Provinces) who delivered a dissenting judgment which sowed the seed for judicial activism in India in 1893. He subscribed to the full to Montesquieu's dictum (*Pensee* I,I95) 'to know modern times, one must know antiquity and each law must be followed in the spirit of all the ages.'

It was a case of an under trial who could not afford to engage a lawyer. So the question was whether the Court could decide his case by merely looking at his papers. Justice Syed Mahmood held that the pre-condition of the case being 'heard' would be fulfilled only when somebody speaks. He, in a case *Queen-Empress* v. *Pobpi and others* held that an appeal under section 420 of the Code of Criminal Procedure could not be disposed of in the absence of the accused and the appellant must be heard in person.[1]

From 1950 to 1980, the Courts in India had assumed the role of the protector of fundamental rights-sentinel of the people's rights. But later, it assumed the role of saviour, of peoples' rights and this role was supported by the people of India.

Legislature and Judicial Activism

It was felt that the Judiciary for some years has been willing to jump into the arena of executive or legislative functions. There appears to be a general agreement that in recent years the Indian Supreme Court has brought out more far reaching changes than the legislature and executive combined. Judicial activism, in fact, is not a distinctly separate concept from usual judicial activities. The expression 'activism', lexically as well as in ordinary parlance, means 'being active', 'doing things with decision' and the expression 'activist' should mean 'one' who favours intensified activities. In this sense every judge is, or at least, should be an activist, as Justice Krishna Iyer observed, "Every judge is an activist either on the forward gear or on the reverse".[2]

Judicial policy making can be either an activity in support of the legislative and executive policy choices or in opposition to them. But, it is the latter pattern of activity that is usually styled as judicial activism and not policy making as such. Judicial activism helps in policy making. In fact it is legislature which should make policy. The essence of true judicial activism is the rendering of decisions which are in tune with the temper and tempo of the times. When the representative government bogs down in failure or inaction, then judiciary should take up its role in correcting the representative government or direct the government in power. According to Upendra Baxi, if the executive or legislature defaults on its legal and constitutional obligations, the court cannot for long take a view, because violations of rights involved in such defaults are of no concerns to them. What, therefore, emerges is that province of judicial function can be construed only in the context of the work being done by the other branches of the government.

During the first decade of functioning of government, political stalwarts from executive and parliament were doing their functions efficiently, but judiciary was understandably inclined to go along with the executive to the farthest extent possible. In the 50s and half through the 70s, the Supreme Court on the whole adopted a judicial and structural view of the Constitution. The Emergency reduced the apex court and High Courts virtually to an arm of the authoritarian executive. However, two years before the declaration of the Emergency, the Supreme Court had handed down the famous decision in the *Kesavanada Bharti*[3] case that the Executive had no right to tamper with the Constitution and alter its basic features. But it remained a passive spectator when Mrs. Gandhi did exactly that. After the end of the Emergency, the Supreme Court and also some of the High Courts began to show signs of judicial activism. They began to intervene in executive as well as legislative areas albeit cautiously. People reposed faith in judicial system because they had no other alternative. May be because of this there are so many cases pending in courts. In 2014, there are over 2 crores cases pending in lower courts. A Parliamentary Committee observes that it is due to shortage of 3,000 judicial personnel. The present table gives state-wise pending cases in state High Courts in 2009.

Table 1: Top ten States with pending Cases in High Courts

States	*Pending cases as on 31-03-2009*
Uttar Pradesh	9, 35, 425
Tamil Nadu	4, 62, 009
Maharashtra	3, 39, 921
West Bengal	3, 06, 253
Punjab & Haryana	2, 47, 115
Orissa	2, 43, 146
Rajasthan	2, 35, 824
Madhya Pradesh	1, 86, 422
Andhra Pradesh	1, 73, 454
Karnataka	1, 32, 308

Source: Supreme Court of India

Quoted in *India Today*, September 7, 2009, p. 23

Table 2: Top ten States with pending cases in District Courts

States	*Pending Cases as on 31-03-2009*
Uttar Pradesh	52, 36, 738
Maharashtra	41, 33, 273
West Bengal	24, 62, 430
Gujarat	22, 42, 686
Bihar	14, 42, 580
Rajasthan	13, 33, 601
Karnataka	10, 82, 342
Madhya Pradesh	10, 73, 955
Tamil Nadu	10, 57, 141
Delhi	10, 27, 585

Source: Supreme Court of India.

Quoted in *India Today*, September 7, 2009, p. 23.

Today the number of pending cases in various High Courts and subordinate courts on September 30, 2010, has gone up to 32, 170, 973. In the apex court alone, the number of case pending as of June 2011 was 57, 179. The United Progressive Alliance (UPA) government promised that by December 31, 2012 most of the cases will be resolved.

Judicial Activism in Action

It was only in the 80s judiciary started taking up public litigation cases seriously. The first major case of judicial activism was the Bihar under trials case. Again in 1980, two Professors of law wrote a letter to the Editor, *Indian Express* describing barbaric conditions of detention in the Agra Protective Home, the basis for a writ petition under Article 21. This was followed by a similar petition for Delhi Women's Home by a third year law student in Delhi Law Faculty and a social worker. Then three journalists after exposing of a thriving market, in which women were bought and sold as cattle, filed a writ petition demanding prohibition of this practice and immediate relief for their victims through programmes of compensation and rehabilitation.

The Supreme Court began to take the cognizance of custody deaths, bride burning and rape in police stations, scams etc. It ordered the police not to handcuff a man arrested purely on suspicion. It ordered that no woman can be taken to a police station after dusk. High Court judges began to visit prisons to check the living conditions of prisoners. In about a single month of 1993, the Supreme Court delivered judgments protecting the rights of innocents held in *Hazaratbal* mosque in Srinagar, defining the constitutional powers of the Chief Election Commissioner, threatening multi-crore rupees industries with closure if they continued to pollute the *Ganga*[4] and endanger the *Taj Mahal*[5] and brought all government and semi-government bodies under the purview of the Consumer-Protection Act.

The P.V. Narshimha Rao Government referred to the Supreme Court the emotive and highly controversial issue of 27 per cent reservation of Jobs in Central Government and Public Sector Undertakings. The court found the decision of the National Front Government constitutionally valid, but exempted the 'creamy layer' from the benefit of the affirmative action. It ordered that creamy layer to be removed first. 'Mean-test' signifies imposition of an income limit for the purpose of excluding persons from the backward classes. Those whose income is above that limit are referred to as the 'creamy layer.' Income or the extent of property can be taken as a measure of social advancement and on that basis the creamy layer of a given caste can be excluded.[6] On the question of extent of reservation, the court decided that altogether 49 per cent of Jobs could be reserved for deprived and poor castes and classes. It also said that reservation cannot go more than 50 per cent in any case. In another decision, the court completely changed the operation of the dreaded capitation fee colleges used in India especially in Karnataka.

The judicial activism was inevitable as the credibility of the Government's investigative agencies-particularly the CBI—had been fatally eroded over the years because they protected the strong and the moneyed through a variety of tactics of delay and technical evasion while the less fortunate rotted in jails for petty offences without even a trial date in sight. Until recently the CBI, in what critics believed was strategy aimed at absolving P.V. Narasimha Rao, held the view that the Prime Minister could not be subjected to scrutiny because the agency's investigation was based on the Jain diary entries alone and not on the oral statement in which he implicated P.V. Narshimha Rao. But nowhere on the record has the Supreme Court stated that the CBI should limit its inquiry to any single source.

On April 2, 1996 the Supreme Court made the Chiefs of Central Investigating Agencies personally answerable regarding investigations into criminal, income tax and FERA offences alleged to have been committed by the controversy god man Chandraswami.[7] Even the court pulled up the CBI for dragging investigations in St. Kitts case and said that if the situation was reached where no candid result could be achieved in the probe the Court may be forced to record a finding that the investigating machinery in the country had come to a grinding halt.[8] On March 20, 1996 the Supreme Court gave a green signal for a CBI probe into Animal Husbandry Scam in Bihar under supervision and control of the Patna High Court.[9] The number of cases that courts have taken up concerning executive and legislative matters and delivered judgments has increased. The courts also have taken seriously the matter of human rights and directed to states. Today court also has taken up matter of 2G spectrum scam and brought the ministers within the purview of court. In the recent case of food insecurity in India the Supreme Court has directed the government to distribute the food item to poor. It has said that in any case food should not go in waste.

The orders and decisions of the Courts in many matters have contributed to the new trend of what is now called, 'Judicial Activism' and thereby informed its critics to accuse the judiciary of playing to the gallery for making a stand on environmental issue. Reacting on this issue M.C. Mehta said, "The dynamism of an institution is an indication of its responsiveness and effectiveness. When the executive fails in its constitutional duties and is considered to be suffering from executive inactivism, there is no other recourse for the people but to turn to the judiciary. If this is perceived as judicial activism, then it is the rope which a citizen in distress can hold on to and hope to be saved. If the judiciary were to remain a mute spectator to contemporary events, it will become a vestigial institution."[10]

Judicial Activism: A Long Way to Go

Today courts are involved in various matters and there are so many cases pending in High Courts and the Supreme Court. Courts are overburdened with many cases. How the cases can be resolved soon is a million dollar question.

Today there are only 26 judges in Supreme Court and many cases are to be resolved. The Supreme Court needs more judges to resolve the cases. There are thirty one sanctioned strength judges in Supreme Court. Former Chief Justice of Supreme Court, Justice S. H. Kapdia said, "Judicial activism and judicial restraint were two facts of courts' functioning. He is also said, "If judicial activism goes beyond a point, then it is against the principle of judicial restraint". He opined that "judicial activism beyond a point is against the rule of law".[11] These cases are not only in Supreme Court. There many more cases in lower courts and High Courts. These are to be resolved very soon. They expect many more cases to come either in the form of writ petition of paper publication or through post cards. In exceptional cases, the Court declared, even a postcard sent by a poor helpless person sent to the court could be admitted as a petition for a writ.

The scope and dimensions of public interest litigation went on increasing-quantitatively and varied issues and problems which should have and could have been solved either by an executive action or by legislative enactments came up before the Court and the courts applied their minds and passed orders. If one recalls, two professors of law write a letter to the Editor, Indian Express describing the barbaric conditions of detention in the Agra Protective Home, which became the basis for the writ petition under Article 21. In order to resolve the cases the courts have started the *mahalok adalat* in different parts of India. People are called to one place to settle the cases. This is the good beginning of settling the cases If one takes the cases in different parts of India one sees that there are number of cases not yet resolved.

Till 2008, in Kandhamal district of Orissa there was 828 cases, out of which 790 cases were found genuine. Around 475 cases have had charge sheets filed. It was targeted that by 2013 end remaining charge sheet will be done. Many cases have been settled. In the State of Gujarat, many cases being retried by fast-track courts.

In 1989 there were 886 cases in Bhagalpur district of Bihar. The trial began 12 years ago. So far 278 have been charge sheeted. There are 31 cases pending. 347 convictions in 10 years since trial began.[12]

Today the Supreme Court under its judicial activism started reading not only the fundamental Rights of Citizens mentioned in chapter III of the constitution but also taking cognizance of many of the non-justifiable directive principles into the fundamental rights and made them enforceable. According to former Chief Justice of Supreme Court J.S. Verma, "Judicial activism is only possible in that country where democracy and rule of law prevailed. It is the duty of the court to come forward whenever public interest is not secured by the act of legislature or executive." Supreme Court judge A.K. Ganguly said that "no government wants a strong judiciary."[13]

According to Justice M.S. Ratnaparkhi, a retired judge, 'the three decades of the Republic brought the Indian society to an impasse where they found that the executive became important, because its political masters wanted it to be so. The legislature became devoid of teeth, because in it is the politicians who constitute the legislature. People in India got convinced that they would not get help either from the legislature or from the executive.... Two wings of the sovereignty became paralysed not because of their inherent defect, but because their political masters did want them to be paralysed for their (master's) political and personal benefits.... There was only one outlet open, and that is the Judiciary.... People reposed faith in judicial system because they had no other alternative.[14]

We hope that judicial Activism will come as a saviour for all, executive, legislature and especially poor masses. There is no doubt that judicial activism is to be considered as a vanguard of Indian Parliamentary democracy. It has been protecting our democracy and will continue its supreme task.

Endnotes

1. F.B. Justice Syed Mahmood as the first Indian Judge in the N.W.P. High Court (now the Allahabad High Court). also see, Fadia, B. L. (1997) 'Indian Government and Politics', Agra: Sahitya Bhawan Publication, p. 833.
2. *Ibid.*, p. 833.
3. Kesavanand Bharati vs The State of Kerala, AIR 1973, SC 1461.
4. M.C. Mehta vs Union of India and others, W.P. (Civil) No. 3727, 1985.
5. M.C. Mehta vs Union of India, 1996 (4) SCALE (SP) 29.
6. *Indra Sawhney vs. Union of India,* (1992) Supp. (3) S.C. 217. Parliament has enacted the National Commission for Backward Classes Act, 1993, to set up a National commission for backward classes.
7. *The Hindustan Times* (New Delhi) April 3, 1996.
8. *The Hindustan Times* (New Delhi) April 13, 1996.
9. *The Hindustan Times* (New Delhi) March 20, 1996
10. Mehta, M. C. "Judicial Activism", *in survey of the environment* 96, The Hindu, Madras, p. 205
11. The *Indian Express* (Mumbai), May 3, 2010.
12. The *Indian Express*, (Nagpur Edition), February 2, 2011.
13. The *Indian Express* (Nagpur Edition), February 12, 2011.
14. Ratnaparkhi, M.S. "Is Judicial Activism—The only Alternative?" The *Hitavada*, (Nagpur Daily), March, 23, 1997.

9

Socio-Political Dimensions of Violence in India

Introduction

Indian history speaks of persons who renounced violence and also had been the great votary of non-violence. Buddha in his eight-fold path has propagated the concept of non-violence. Mahavira, a contemporary of Gautam Buddha and propagator of Jainism, was the exponent of non-violence which embraced all living creatures. In 20th century, Mahatma Gandhi was the practitioner of non-violence and with this weapon, he fought against British government for India' freedom.

Violence generally signifies an attack or an assault resulting in destructive consequences. The Webster dictionary defines violence as an act of extreme force or passion or fierceness. This view construes that the act of violence is primarily physical and focuses on intense emotions that incite violence. However, violence is pervasive. Violence happens every where–in street, in public transport, at work place and also at home. No country, city or community is immune or untouched to it. Violence can be perpetrated by strangers, by groups, communities, states, or even people known to victims. Violence is a very complex phenomenon. It is governed by prevalent social norms which are constantly changing and prescribe what is acceptable or unacceptable.

Violence is elusive, complex and multidimensional. Violence is the application of force which results in injury or destruction of persons.

In common parlance violence is understood as willful application of such force in such a way that it physically or psychologically injures or causes damage to person, group or property against whom it is applied. Actually the dynamics of violence has long been a preoccupation of the social scientists of all ideological persuasion. Violence is a term that suffers from a surfeit of meanings. Even a cursory glance through the rapidly growing literature on the subject is enough to show the bewildering melody in which the concept is entrapped. The dictionary meaning of violence is the exercise of physical force so as to inflict injury or damage to persons or property. The violence is an act of a person, which encroaches upon the freedom of another. Any case, it infringes the rights of other human beings. Margaret has defined violence as the unsanctioned damage to person or property.[1] All violence as such is not condemnable. It may be for the interest of human existence. In fact 'violence is violence only in the form of and unsanctioned damage to persons or property'. Violence is also man's struggle to adapt to his environment.[2]

According to Random House Dictionary of English Language, "*violence means rough or injurious physical force, action or treatment.*" In other words, it is the expression of aggressive drives on personal and social levels. "*Personal violence is a violent act of a man or woman against another man or woman—such as assault and rape, homicide.*" On the other hand, genocide, concentration camps, communal riots refer to social violence. Some scholars try to relate violence with aggression. Daniels has different view in this regard. Daniels says that 'aggression' is entire spectrum of assertive, intrusive and attacking behaviour. Violence, as a specialised sub-form of aggression, is accompanied by the emotion of anger or hostility; and anger occurs when a plan of action towards a valued goal is interrupted by interference specific enough to warrant attack[3] or "when the expected rewards for attack override other outcomes."[4]

Encyclopedia of the Social Sciences[5] says that in the social context violence may be defined roughly as the illegal employment of methods of physical coercion for personal or group ends. It is distinct from force or power, which is a purely physical concept.

Violence manifests itself in the form of creating law and order situation, beating up people, wrecking cars, breaking into shops and clubs causing extensively senseless damage; indulging in hooliganism; fights among the teenagers and young people; burning of buses and other public property, cinemas, college furniture, etc. youth violence ranges from "eve-teasing" and "*goondaism*" to rioting, and national and communal violence. Violence can be of different forms. It can be social violence, communal violence, sexual violence etc.

In this chapter an effort is made to study socio-political dimensions of violence. Primarily, an attempt is made to study the communal violence in India. Communal violence has political connotation whereas domestic violence has social connotations. Effort is made delve the communal violence in India and then study societal violence.

Communalism and Communal Violence in India

Scholars have tried to define communalism in different ways. Some view it as an ideology which emphasises the separate identity of a religious group in relation to other groups and often a tendency to promote of its own interest at their expense. Adherence to a religion or religious system is not only communalism. At the same time attachment to any religious community cannot be considered communalism. Indulgence in ritualism, superstition, obscurantism, belief in astrology cannot be a matter of communalism. Communalism means the opposition of religious communities of each other. On the other hand using a religious community against other communities and against the nation is communalism. It is an ideology which emphasises the separate identity of a religious group in relation to other groups, may be linguistic group, caste group, and regional group and sometime it has a tendency to promote its own interest at their expense. The relationship between two groups becomes hostile and then problem starts and then antagonistic posture of the group itself becomes a substitute for religious and leads to clashes in society.

Once Jawaharlal Nehru, first Prime Minister of Independent India had rightly pointed out that the greatest danger for this country is from communalism and not so much from external aggression because when there is external aggression, the people of India tend to get united but when communalism is rampant the people get divided. Communalism is, thus, the most deadly enemy of the people of India.

According to V.R. Mehta, a well known Political Scientist, Nationalism and communalism have been the most important factors of the root of major crisis in twentieth century Indian politics. Nationalism has been the aspiration and communalism the disease and both in their ways have shaped Indian Politics.[6]

According to Bipin Chandra, an expert on modern history, "the concept of communalism is based on the belief that religious distinction is the most important and fundamental distinction, and this distinction overrides all other distinctions. Some Hindus, Muslims and Sikhs are different religious entities; their social, economic, cultural and political interests are also dissimilar and divergent. As such the loss of one religious group is the gain of another group and vice-versa. If a particular community seeks to better its social and economic situation, it is doing at the expense of the other."[7]

Communalism and communal violence are two different connotations. In many cases Communal ideology leads to communal violence and riots. Communal ideology is primary and the cause, but communal violence is the consequence. Rioting, looting and killing and other forms of communal violence are contingent or conjectural forms of communal thinking. Communal violence is a consequence of the spread of communal thinking or religious dogmas. Communal riot and its cruelty, viciousness, inhumanity, beastliness and barbarity and its toll of many dead and large-scale of destruction of property hits the headlines in Gujarat, Uttar Pradesh, Bihar, Maharashtra and Orissa and these have compelled us to study the situations. No doubt communal violence acts as a means of spreading communal ideology and religious dogma. Gujarat violence of February-March 2002 which horrified the entire nation, was the consequence of the prior spread of communal ideology or way of thinking through BJP's and RSS's propaganda machinery, school textbooks, etc., for several years.[8] Today, effort is made to include *goga, surya namaskar*, and religious text as a part of syllabus. Similarly, in Orissa, spread of communal ideology led to the communal violence. Here, the communal violence was between Hindus and Christians. On the other hand in Gujarat, the communal violence was between two religious groups, Hindus and Muslims.

Since independence many communal violence have taken place in India. From 1954 to 1963 there were average of 62 communal violence and riots annually and the number of those killed is around 40 per year. Again from 1964 to 1970 the country had an average of 425 communal riots and average of 467 killed each year. From 1971 to 1978 the average number of riots came down 234 and the average number of persons killed to 68. It can be said that the more than 50 per cent of serious cases of communal riots and violence in India are due to inaction, orally ordered by government.

According to the Home Ministry data between 2001 and 2009 6,541 communal clashes occurred and 2,234 persons were killed. Though the number of communal clashes may be correct officially the number of casualties is never reported accurately in official records for various reasons. In 2002 in Gujarat alone, all non-official sources agree, was 2000 dead and official sources are showing number of deaths between 2001 and 2009 i.e., over a period of 8 years as 2,234 i.e., minus Gujarat total number of dead over a period of 8 years in all only 234 persons died which can hardly be accurate. But if we take official figure of dead in Gujarat riots of 2002 as 1000, then over a period of 8 years 1234 people died i.e., more than 150 people per year which is not so small, after all.[9] The communal violence has been continuing every parts of India. Christians are being attacked on the pretext of conversion everywhere. Today there are number of cases of anti-Christian movement in India. There has been number of attacks on Christian churches in Delhi, Haryana, Navi Mumbai and many other States of Indian Union. The rape of 71 year old nun in West Bengal has raised doubt about the security of minuscule minority. Still it would be too early to give communal colour to this incident.

Communal Violence

India is a multi religious country. Some religions were born in India. No religion teaches violence. Still violence and riot free India remains a distant dream. Communalism, communal politics, assumes that people belonging to one religion have similar interests and these are opposed to the interests of the people belonging to 'other' religions. In its milder form it asserts that interests of the people belonging to one religion are similar. In moderate form, it goes on to state that these interests of one community are different from the interests of the 'other' community' and in its severe form it asserts that these are opposed to the ones of other community.

During our freedom struggle these communal trends, manifested in the form of Muslim League and Hindu Mahasabha, RSS. Muslim League, with this understanding wanted an Islamic state (Pakistan) and the Hindu Mahasabha-RSS stated that it is a Hindu Rashtra. Both these streams had no popular support. These outfits were essentially representing the interests of the Landlord-Clergy who were feeling threatened by the rising struggle for India's freedom due to the coming up of Dalits and women in the social and political space. India's struggle for freedom was an ensemble of three basic processes. One, drive away the British colonial powers. Two, build India as a nation state. And, three bring in caste and gender equality. This period saw all the three components of the movement going on hand in hand. This was the period when Dalits started coming to the social space. The movements led by Jotiba P.hule and Bhimrao Ambedkar amongst others in this direction aimed to bring in social justice for the vast mass of untouchables, the downtrodden. The movements initiated by Savitribai Phule and later on the travails of Pandita Ramabai set the trend for women striving for an equal status in society. Savitribai Phule promoted education for women who were not allowed earlier. The spirit of freedom struggle did get enshrined in the Indian Constitution.

Communal Violence in Post-Independent Period

Communal violence is the festering wound on the body politic of Indian society. In pre-independence period the communal riots were a sort of reciprocal violence between Hindus and Muslims with the police (mainly British officers) intervening to restore peace. The nature of these riots after independence has changed in a significant way. First, the number of victims is more from Muslim community, second, the loss of property is also more of Muslims and third, police plays a heavily partisan role in favour of the majority community. Initially it used to be mainly the poor Muslims who were the major victims, but lately even the middle and upper class Muslims have also been drawn into this vortex. Today Christians are also the target of attack on the pretext of conversion.

The post-partition riots were followed by a period of comparative calm, in the decade of 50s, barring the one episode in eastern India and East Pakistan in 1950. This calm was broken in 60s when in 1962 and 1964 Jabalpur, Jamshedpur and Rourkela riots broke out. "Of the bloody pogroms in sixties, the ones at Ranchi, Bihar (1962) and Ahmedabad, Gujarat (1969) stand out as the major events. In seventies the Turkman Gate massacre of 1976 perpetrated by police...., the riots in Moradabad (1980), Nellie, Naogaon, Assam (1983), Bhiwandi (1984) and Meerut (1987) have been the major ones in which more than a thousand lost their lives" (Khalidi, 1995). The Ramjanmabhumi campaign left a big trail of blood in which more than thousand people lost their lives in 1989. The massacres of Bhagalpur, Hydrabad and Aligarh heralded the onset of bloody 80s, which has seen the peak of communal violence.

Post-Babri demolition riots of 1996 was one of the worst, the country has suffered so far. The post demolition riots gripped Mumbai, Surat, and Bhopal in a major way and many other places in a significant way. From 1960 to 1995 the incidences of riots have been on an upswing. A big proportion of these have been taking place in six states UP, Gujarat, Rajasthan, Bihar, Madhya Pradesh and Assam. The violence has been also been taking place in North-east states. But violence in these States is not communalised much. Violence in these States have different outlook. Present table gives the detailed-communal violence in our post-independent time.

Table 1: Communal Violence since independence

Name/Place	*Date*	*Location*	*Death*	*Notes*
Partition of India	1947	Punjab	1 Million both sides	Massacre of Sikhs and Hindus by Muslims in West Punjab and of Muslims by Sikhs and Hindus in East Punjab.
Hyderabad massacre of 1948	1948	Hyderabad	27-40,000 killed	Massacre of Muslims.
1969 Gujarat riots	1969	Gujarat	Total 660	Hindu-Muslim riots, 430 Muslims died.
Turkman gate demolition and rioting	1976	Delhi	Officially 6, unofficially 150 killed	Killing of Delhi residents who refused to move residence.
Marichjhapi incident	1979	West Bengal	Official figures 2, Hindustan Times quotes 50 to 1000	Killing of refugees who came from East Pakistan.
Moradabad riots	1980	Uttar Pradesh	Officially 400; un-official estimates as high as 2500.	Started as a Muslim-Police conflict; later turned into a Hindu-Muslim riot.
Mandai massacre	1980	Tripura	255-500 Bengali Hindu refugees.	
Nellie massacre	1983	Assam	2,191 muslims	
Train Passenger massacre	23 Feb. 1984	Punjab	11 Hindu	
1984 anti-Sikh riots	1984	Delhi	2,700-4,000 (nearly all Sikhs).	After Assassination of Indira Gandhi by her Sikh bodyguards.
Hondh-Chillar massacre	1984	Hondh-Chillar, Haryana	32 Sikhs	After Assassination of Indira Gandhi by her Sikh bodyguards.
Desri Ground massacre	1986	Ludhiana Punjab	13 Hindus	
Mallian massacre	Mar. 1986	Jalandhar, Punjab	20 Hindu Labourers	

(Cont...)

Bus Passenger massacre	July 1986	Mukatsar, Punjab	15 Hindus	
Bus Passenger massacre	Nov. 1986	Khudda, Punjab	24 Hindus	
Hashimpura massacre	22 May 1987	Meerut, Uttar Pradesh	42 Muslims	
Bus Passenger massacre	July 1987	Fatehbad, Haryana	80 Hindus	
Jagdev Kalan massacre	Aug. 1987	Punjab	13 Hindus	
Rajbah massacre	Mar. 1987	Punjab	18 Hindus belonging to 1 family	
Bhagalpur riots	1989	Bhagalpur, Bihar	1,070 mostly Muslims	More than 50,000 Muslims were displaced from their ancestral homes.
Ethnic cleansing of Hindu Pandits	1990s	Kashmir	219-399	140,000 to 192,000 Hindus were forced to abandon their ancestral land.
Gawakadal massacre	20 Jan. 1990	Srinagar, Kashmir	35 Muslims	Firing on procession by Indian CRPF.
Rajbah massacre	31 Mar. 1988	Punjab	18 Hindus belonging to 1 family	
Train Passenger massacre II	15 June 1988	Ludhiana, Punjab	80 Mostly Hindus	
Train Passenger massacre III	Dec. 1988	Ludhiana, Punjab	49 (mostly Hindus)	
Bombay Riots	Dec.1992-Jan. 1993	Mumbai	575 Muslims, 275 Hindus, 45 unknown and 5 others.	Firing on procession by Indian CRPF.
Sopore Massacre	6 Jan. 1993	Sopore, Kashmir	55 Muslims	Firing on procession by Indian BSF.

(Cont...)

Laxmanpur Bathe massacre	1 Dec. 1997	Arwal district, Bihar	58	Upper caste Ranvir Sena enter village at night and kill 58 *Dalits*.
Wandhama massacre	25 Jan. 1998	Wandhama,Jammu and Kashmir	23 Hindus	Terrorist groups
Prankote massacre	17 April 1998	Jammu and Kashmir	26 Hindus	
Chapnari massacre	19 June 1998	Chapnari, Jammu and Kashmir	25 Hindus	Terrorist groups
Chamba massacre	3 Aug. 1998	Chamba district, Himachal Pradesh	35 Hindus	Communal Riots
Chittisinghpura massacre	20 Mar. 2000	Chittisinghpura, Anantnag district, Jammu and Kashmir	36 Sikhs	Terrorist Groups
Gourangatilla massacre	2000	Tripura	16 non-tribal Hindus	By Christian extremist
Bagber massacre	20 May. 2000	Tripura	25 non-tribal Hindus	By Christian extremist
Tripura Tribal massacre	1999-2000	Tripura	20 tribal Hindus	Includes murder of tribal Hindu spiritual leader.
Nanoor massacre	27 July 2000	West Bengal	11 labourers	
Amarnath pilgrimage massacre	1 Aug. 2000	Jammu and Kashmir	30 Hindu pilgrims	Terrorist groups.
Kishtwar massacre	3 Aug. 2001	Jammu and Kashmir	19 Hindus	Terrorist groups.
Godhra train burning	27 Feb. 2002	Godhra*	58 Hindus	Hindu passengers brutally burnt alive in a train fire Courts convicted 31 Muslims 11 to be executed by Hanging and 21 for life in prison.
Gujarat violence	28 Feb. 2002	Ahmedabad	790 Muslims and 254 Hindus were killed	Communal Violence

(Cont...)

Gulbarg Society massacre	28 Feb. 2002	Ahmedabad	69 (mostly Muslim) (21 were Hindus.	
Naroda Patiya massacre	28 Feb. 2002	Naroda, Ahmedabad	97 Muslims	Riots between Hindus and Muslims after Sabarmati Express is set afire at Godhra railway station by Muslims. The Muslim perpetrators have been convicted 11 to be hung and 21 for life.**
Raghunath Hindu temple massacre	30 Mar. 2002	Jammu & Kashmir	11 Hindus brutally killed, 20 injured (Hindu devotees)	Terrorist groups
Qasim Nagar massacre	13 July 2002	Jammu & Kashmir	29 Hindus Killed	Terror Attack
Akshardham Temple attack	24 Sept. 2002	Gujarat	29 killed, 79 injured (Hindu devotees)	Terror Attack
Raghunath Hindu temple massacre	24 Nov. 2002	Jammu & Kashmir	14 killed, 45 injured (mostly Muslim devotees)	
Nadimarg Massacre	23 Mar. 2002	Jammu & Kashmir	24 Hindus	Terrorist Groups
Kaluchak massacre	14 May 2002	Jammu & Kashmir	31	Terrorist groups attack Tourist bus and Army's family quarter attacked
Marad Massacre	May 2003	Kerala	8 killed, 58 injured - All Hindu Fisher-men	Planned Attack by Muslim Group.
Varanasi bombingsz	2006	Uttar Pradesh	28 killed, 101 injured.	Terrorist attack Hindu temple
Doda massacre	30 April 2006	Jammu & Kashmir	35 Hindus	Terrorist groups

(Cont...)

Tumudibandh massacre	Aug. 2008	Orissa	5 Hindus	By Christian extremists
Mumbai massacre	26 Nov. 2008	Mumbai	164	11 coordinated attacks by Lashkar-e-Taiba terrorists; casualties include people of various nationalities, and Israeli victims were reportedly tortured before being killed.
Dantewada bus bombing	17 May 2010	Chhattisgarrh	76	Maoist terrorist attacked civilian bus.
Deganga riots	6 Sept. 2010	North 24 Parganas district, West Bengal	Attack on Hindu by Muslim mobs led by Haji Nurul Islam	23 houses ransacked,250 shops had been looted during the several days of rioting,while 50 houses had been burned and 5 temples desecrated.
Assam violence	July 2012	Assam	77 death	Communal violence between Bodos and Muslims.
Canning riots	21 Feb. 2013	Canning subdivision, West Bengal	Attack on Hindu by Muslim mobs	Burned down over 200 Hindu homes and 24 Hindu-owned shops were looted after a Muslim cleric was killed by unidentified assailants.
Canni Naxal attack in Darbha valleyng riots	25 May 2013	Chhattisgarrh	28	28 people from a Congress Party motorcade.
Muzaffarnagar riots	25 Aug. 2013 - 17 Sept. 2013	Muzaffarnagar district, Uttar Pradesh	42 Muslims and 20 Hindus killed and 93 injured	Double murder of two Hindu boys triggered communal riot between Hindu Jats and Muslim Jatavs.

http://en.wikipedia.org/wiki/List_of_massacres_in_India (Accessed on 23/3/2015)

*http://en.wikipedia.org/wiki/Godhra_train_burning

**http://en.wikipedia.org/wiki/Godhra_train_burning

Communalisation of Violence

This communalisation process goes through various levels, beginning from 'the Muslims are aliens', 'responsible for partition of the country', 'have spread Islam on the strength of sword' and 'are loyal to Pakistan. Sometime, it is felt by majority that Muslims population is increasing. Maharashtra government proposed 5 per cent reservation to Muslims in jobs. That becomes a threat to Hindu majority. On the other hand Christians are converting in the pretext of social service. These have been the allegation of majority in our society. Most of the incidents are given religious colour and subsequently led to communal violence. In this violence poor minority becomes the victim. It goes without saying that Hindu fundamentalists are the main player in this game in today's scenario. It keeps getting stimulation and provocation from the remnants of Muslims communalism whose acts of commission, though feeble in social intensity are pretext enough for Hindu fundamentalist to pounce on the Muslim community with full intensity. After the assassination of Indira Gandhi, country faces another communal violence. Almost 300 Sikh lost their life.

Caste Violence

The caste violence and caste atrocity against scheduled castes are considered as synonymous. The violence against scheduled castes is all organised ones by the upper castes. Atrocities are the "Physical manifestations of violence, crime and such want only cruel acts against the persons and/or property which are illegal in the eye of law. Atrocities on scheduled castes refer to ghastly acts of the higher castes on the lower castes. The recent purification of school in Bhandara district of Maharashtra has shown that caste discrimination still continues in many parts of India. Bhandara district is the hot bed for atrocities against Dalit. In the early April 2007, when new school headmaster named Sharad Kaitade, an upper caste, took over the charge of Zilla Parishad School at Bhandara village he is allegedly performed puja in the school. A lady teacher named Madhavi Raut sprinkeled gomutra (cow urine) in the class and the school premises to purify the school. The students were writing their annual examination. Lady teacher asked the dalit students to get up and sprinkled cow urine on them saying that this would purify them. This is height of ill treatment to dalit in this 21st century.[10] There are numbers of conflicts that is witnessed between the higher castes and scheduled castes.

One of the main reasons for these atrocities is that there is social mobility among scheduled castes. As such scheduled castes are enjoying the fruits of such social movements by gaining the due share and their rightful status. On the other hand it had led to violent caste atrocities and sever class wars between the scheduled castes and higher castes. There are various features of these caste violence..

Firstly, scheduled castes suffer from traditionally low ritual status, which is compounded by appalling poverty and political disenfranchisement. These factors lead to violence and all ill treatment of scheduled castes people. The upper castes take advantages of such multifarious deprivations and provoke violence.

Secondly, the scheduled castes lack high quality of leadership. Atrocities are not the result of single cause but are caused by member of factors such as illiteracy, low wage, forced labour, and non-utilisation of public facilities etc. The atrocities on scheduled castes are predominantly group phenomena.[11]

Thirdly, Government measures for the upliftments of scheduled castes serve as an incentive to jealousy among the non-scheduled castes counterparts. Legal action, Socio-political education and Voluntary bodies support have effect of producing fear and anger among the upper castes.

Fourthly, the caste conflict between the caste Hindus and the scheduled castes in the villages is due to the increasing impact of modernity such as the spread of education, impact of media and increasing politicisation of the lower castes. Because of the politicisation process, the scheduled castes have started asserting their rights and as a result thereof the traditional social order is under attack that is not liked by the higher communities. Because of injured feelings on both sides caste conflicts have taken place at *Belchhi* and *Pipra* in Bihar Sadhulpur in Uttar Pradesh, Kherlangji village in Bhandara district in Maharashtra. There are many more cases where the untouchables are attacked by higher castes.

Societal Violence

The second part of this chapter is devoted on social dimension of violence, the violence which is confined to our house. This may be domestic violence and molestation and rape in our society. In this second part of this chapter, an effort is made to study two types of violence against women in our society. Domestic violence is on the question of dowry. The study is limited to rape cases and dowry death.

Societal violence can be studied from different angles. The present chapter would try to study only societal violence out of many typology of violence in India. Effort is made to study two very important type of violence that is taking place in India. They are Rape as violence and Domestic Violence and Dowry death in India.

Rape cases and Violence against Women

There number of crimes/violence committed against women in India. The Ministry of Home Affairs (Government of India) has brought out the report regarding the crime against women in India. This report reveals the shocking data which speaks of various types of crime committed against women. Women are ill-treated, misbehaved, raped, killed on the issue of dowry and kidnapped in our society in spite of passing an Act of popularly known as Domestic Violence against women, Act 2005. If one sees the one decade data on the crime against women, one finds that there is an increase of crimes against women. (See table no. 2, different types of crimes from 2002 to 2012). There is an increase in all types of crime against women. The graph shows increase of percentage of crimes.

Table 2: Rise and height of crime against women in one decade

Year	*Rape*	*Molestation*	*Sexual Harassment*	*Cruelty by Relatives*	*Abduction*	*Dowry death*	*All crimes*
2012	24,923	45,351	9,173	106527	38262	8233	2,32,469
2011	24,206	42,968	8,570	99,135	35,565	8,618	2,19,062
2010	22,172	40,613	9,961	94,041	29,795	8,391	2,04,973
2009	21,397	38,711	11,009	89,546	25,741	8,383	1,94,787
2008	21,467	40,413	12,214	81,344	22,939	8,172	1,86,549
2007	20,737	38,734	10,950	75,930	20,416	8,093	1,74,860
2006	19,348	36,617	9,966	63,128	17,414	7,618	1,54,091
2005	18,359	34,175	9,984	58,319	15,750	6,787	1,43,374
2004	18,233	43,567	10,001	58,121	15,578	7,026	1,43,526
2003	15,847	32,939	12,325	50,703	13,296	6,208	1,31,318
2002	16,373	33,943	10,155	49,237	14,506	6,822	1,31,036
Total	**1,98,139**	**3,73,680**	**1,05,135**	**7,19,504**	**2,11,000**	**76,118**	**16,83,576**

Source: National Crime Record Bureau, 2002-2012

Though the problem of rape is considered to be serious in all countries, in India it was statistically not as serious as it is in the Western society. In comparison to western countries, the rate in India is 0.5 per one lakh population. Taking into account the number of rape cases in our country between 1990 and 1994, it may be said that there were 30 rapes a day. If one see the age wise rape cases, the percentage of victims of rape is highest in the age group of 16 to 30 years (64 per cent) while victims below 10 years account for about 3 per cent, victims between 10 and 16 years account for about 20 per cent and victims above 30 years account for about 13 per cent.[12] It is not only the poor girls who become rape victims but even the employees belonging to the middle class are sexually humiliated by their employers. Women are humiliated/raped in jail, hospital, and work places. Today the there is a rise in the rape cases in India. For example every 60 minutes, two women are raped in India. What is more horrendous is that 133 elderly women were sexually assaulted last year, according to latest report prepared by the National Crime Records Bureau (NCRB). Live aside the rape case of young girls; today even the women are raped. The NCRB has provided figure of women rape in India too. It says that one of every four crimes against children is rape.[13] A total of 20, 737 cases of rape were reported last year registering a 7.2 per cent increase over the previous year, with Madhya Pradesh becoming the "Rape Capital" of the country. Going by the NCRB statistics, two women are raped in the country every hour. Madhya Pradesh (3,010) accounted for 14.5 per cent of total cases, with West Bengal following with 2, 106 such incidents. Records in other States are Uttar Pradesh (1,648), Bihar (1, 555) and Rajasthan (1,238). The national capital had 598 cases. Among all rapists in national capital 68 per cent were illiterates and school-drop-outs, 24 per cent studied up to class X, 21.9 per cent were graduates and 80 per cent of accused were poor.[14]

Child Rape Case in India

Children are most vulnerable, especially to sexual abuse, because society treats them as non-entities. Children in our culture are brought up with the conditioning that adults know best and they are never wrong. Consequently, the child never learns to say no to an adult and is often docile. Many adults take undue advantage of this situation and exploit children sexually.

In a shocking revelation, a government commissioned survey has found that more than 53 per cent of children in India are subjected to sexual abuse, but most do not report the assaults to anyone. Almost 22 per cent faced severe sexual abuse; around 6 per cent said that they were sexually assaulted. Younger children (5-12 years) face higher level of abuse. Among the states Andhra Pradesh, Bihar and Assam reported highest levels of abuse.[15]

The rape of a child is absolutely shattering for her at a tender age. The traumatic experience invariably causes irreparable physical and psychological damage.

As per 2008 statistic available with Ministry of Home affair (Government of India), Uttar Pradesh tops by registering 900 child rape cases among all Indian states and Union Territories in 2008. According to the latest data available with the Ministry of Home Affairs, for three years, cases of child rape continue to rise as a total of 4, 721 in 2006, 5, 045 in 2007 and 5, 446 in 2008 cross the country.

The statistics of 2008 report of the Ministry of Home Affairs reveals the state-wise rape cases in India. They are: Madhya Pradesh 892, Maharashtra 690, Rajasthan 420, Andhra Pradesh 412, Chhattigarh 411, Delhi 301, Kerala 215, Tamil Nadu 187, West Bengal 129, Punjab 106, Tripura 104, Gujarat 99, Karnataka 97, Bihar 91, Haryana 70, Himachal Pradesh 68, Orissa 65, Goa 18, Arunachal Pradesh 11, Sikkim 12, Mizorum 18, Manipur 22, Assam 27 and 34 in Meghalaya.

Domestic Violence and Dowry Deaths

The second aspect of social violence is domestic violence and dowry death. A bill on domestic violence has been passed in 2005 and it came into effect in 2006. The much-welcomed Act was aimed at giving protection and compensation for all kinds of abuse at home, including physical, sexual, verbal, emotional and economic. The new law requires a sentence to be passed within 90 days of the first hearing. But in many states, implementation of the Protection of Women from Domestic Violence Act (PWDVA) has been abysmally poor. There is a provision for a protection officer in some states who are authorised to help women get speedy justice. The existing protection officers are over burdened with work and are reluctant to take on additional responsibilities. What has also led many women to suffer in silence is the existence of corrupt police personal, a shortage of state sponsored medical and shelter facilities and non-access to legal aid in states such as Maharashtra, Tamil Nadu, Bihar and Arunachal Pradesh. In Uttar Pradesh, women are made to pay for paper work and the visits of protection officers and bribes are often given by offenders to get them absolved of their crimes.[16]

The Delhi Government has appointed 17 protection Officers in all districts of the state under the domestic violence law. "Though the Delhi Government has appointed protection officers, their numbers are very few", said a Criminal lawyer in Delhi.[17]

The capital's west district recorded the highest number of domestic violence cases at 844 followed by 613 cases in the north district and 37 in the New Delhi district. Delhi alone has recorded a whopping 3, 901 cases possibly the highest in the country. Besides Capital of India others states also have high record of domestic violence. States like, Kerala 3,287 cases, Chhatisgarh 2,921, Maharashtra 2,751, Punjab 2017, Andhra Pradesh 1,625. Delhi Records 3,900 cases of domestic violence against Women.[18]

According to the National Family Health Survey III, 37.2 per cent Indian married women experience violence and abuse their spouse. Among the states with widest prevalence of domestic violence are Bihar, with 62.2 per cent urban cases and 58.5 per cent rural, Rajasthan 46.3 per cent, Madhya Pradesh 45.8 per cent and Uttar Pradesh 42.4 per cent.[19] It would be noteworthy to study the implementation of Protection of Women from Domestic Violence Act (PWDVA). According to a report by Lawyers Collective, a non-profit legal organisation, 7,913 applications were filed under the Act as of July 31, 2007, with the maximum cases from Rajasthan 3,440, followed by Kerala 1,028, Andhra Pradesh 731 and Delhi 607. It seems that maximum number of domestic violence is done in Rajasthan. What is the reply to this application that one has to wait and watch?

The dowry death and domestic violence was very common in north India. It seemed that a plague was spreading across most Indian cities and an increasing number of urban, educated, middle class women were falling prey to it. The ultimate manifestation of the decease was a charred body of a young bride. The cause of death was being identified as 'dowry'. Dowry deaths either by way of suicide by a harassed wife or murder by the greedy husband and in-laws have become a serious concern for all. The newspapers almost give the news of dowry death every day.

In the wake of the public protests against these deaths, it came to be accepted, both nationally as well as internationally, that women in India were being subjected to a culture specific violence termed as 'dowry violence', which eventually culminated into a 'dowry death'. Further, it was explained that increasing consumerism and avarice by husbands and in-laws was the root cause of this problem. Dowry deaths were providing the husband a convenient outlet to get rid of one wife and find another, with even more dowry. But rather fortunately, society is not divided into two clear and mutually exclusive categories of parents – those of the boys, the dowry takers and the other of girls, the dowry givers. On the contrary, in most cases, the boy's parents, the dowry takers also happen to be the dowry givers, the girl's parents. This renders the theory of consumerism, avarice and greed as the root cause of dowry and dowry related violence seemed a little too far fetched. Though the dowry Prohibition Act, 1961 has banned the practice of dowry but still the dowry death continues.

Conclusion

The BJP is in power in a few states and it is going all out to promote RSS agenda in these states and also to recruit people with the RSS background which itself is great danger to our secularism. The Congress is the only national party with secular ideology but is not honest as it should be in fighting menace of communalism.

Otherwise there is no reason why India cannot be riot-free. Violence against minorities continues. As Jawaharlal Nehru said, that the greatest danger for India is from communalism and not from external forces. It is the duty of all parties to come out of their party ideology and fight against communal violence.

Caste violence, domestic violence against women and dowry death still exist in our India society. In spite of many legislations social violence has become like a deadly cancer, which hallows our society. It is a parasite, which has a vice like grip over the body politic of the vast country. There were many saints, mahatmas and social activists, social reformers, who tried their best to introduce schemes for the upliftment of bottom heap of society. And obviously education is one of the potent antidotes to combat this menace. Empowerment and enfranchisement are the master keys to be operationalised towards this goal. And again Education is the only way through which women can be liberated from this evil. The NGOs can contribute a lot in this direction. In fact the resources and intellectual capital of entire civic society needs deployment to create just and equitable society. The road is littered with all sorts of minefields but battle must be engaged. Other wise social chaos and disintegration would swallow one and all. It is the prime duty of all responsible citizens to fight against all types of violence and make India a violence free nation.

Endnotes

1. Mahendra Kumar, 1975: Violence and Non-violence in International Relations, Thomson Press (India), p. 46.
2. *Ibid.*, p. 47.
3. D.N. et al. Daniels, 1970: Violence and the Struggle for Existence, Little Brown and Company, Boston, p. 98.
4. *Ibid.*, p. 14.
5. Hook, Sidney, 1935: *Violence, In Encyclopedia of the Social Sciences, (ed)* Vol. 15, Macmillan Company, New York, p. 264.
6. V.R. Mehta, Ideology, Modernisation and Politics in India, Manohar Publishing House, New Delhi, 1983, p. 153.

7. Bipin Chandra, *Communalism in India*, People's Publishing House, New Delhi. 1981, p. 2. Also see Bipin Chandra, Communalism A Primer, Anamika Publication, New Delhi, 2004, p. 7.
8. Teesta Setalvad, "How Textbooks teach Prejudice," *Social Action*, October-December, 2000, Vol. 50. No. 4, pp. 384-363.
9. Asghar Ali Engineer, (2011), Social Perspective, Centre for Study of Society and Secularism, Mumbai.
10. "Panel to probe Bhandara purification incident," *The Times of India* (Nagpur edition), April 27, 2007.
11. "Where Power Flows from the Barrel of the Gun" *Indian Express* (New Delhi) July 17, 1986.
12. *Crime in India,* 1992.
13. Mihir Srivastava, "Mind of a Rapist," *India Today*, July 6, 2009, p. 40.
14. Op. cit., *India Today,* July 6, 2009, p. 40.
15. "53 per cent Indian Kids Sexually Abused", *Times of India* (Nagpur Edition), April 10, 2007.
16. Taru Bahl, "Why the Domestic Violence Act is not helping Women", *Hitavada,* (Nagpur daily), April 1, 2009.
17. *Hitavada*, (Nagpur daily), June 29, 2009.
18. *Ibid.*
19. Op.cit., *Hitavada* (Nagpur daily) April 1, 2009.

Appendix

THE COMMISSIONS FOR PROTECTICTION OF CHILD RIGHTS ACT, 2005

No. 4 of 2006

[20January. 2006.]

An Act to provide for the constitution of a National Commission and State Commissions for Protection of Child Rights and Children's Courts for providing speedy trial of offences against children or of violation of child rights and for matters connected therewith or incidental thereto.

WHEREAS India participated in the United Nations (UN) General Assembly Summit in 1990, which adopted a Declaration on Survival, Protection and Development of Children;

AND WHEREAS India has also acceded to the Convention on the Rights of the Child (CRC) on the 11th December, 1992;

AND WHEREAS CRC is an international treaty that makes it incumbent upon the signatory States to take all necessary steps to protect children's rights enumerated in the Convention;

AND WHEREAS in order to ensure protection of rights of children one of the recent initiatives that the Government have taken for Children is the adoption of National Charter for Children, 2003;

AND WHEREAS the UN General Assembly Special Session on Children held in May, 2002 adopted an Outcome Document titled "A World Fit for Children" containing the goals, objectives, strategies and activities to be undertaken by the member countries for the current decade;

AND WHEREAS it is expedient to enact a law relating to children to give effect to the policies adopted by the Government in this regard, standards prescribed in the CRC, and all other relevant international instruments;

BE it enacted by Parliament in the Fifty-sixth Year of the Republic of India as follows:—

Chapter I

Preliminary

1. (1.) This Act may be called the Commissions for Protection of Child Rights Act, 2005.

(2.) It extends to the whole of India except the State of Jammu and Kashmir.

(3.) It shall come into force on such date as the Central Government may, by notification in the Official Gazette, appoint.

2. In this Act, unless the context otherwise requires,—

(a) "Chairperson" means the Chairperson of the Commission or of the State Commission, as the case may be;

(b) "Child rights" includes the children's rights adopted in the United Nations convention on the Rights of the Child on the 20th November, 1989 and ratified by the Government of India on the 11th December, 1992;

(c) "Commission" means the National Commission for Protection of Child Rights constituted under section 3;

(d) "Member" means a Member of the Commission or of the State Commission, as the case may be, and includes the Chairperson;

(e) "Notification" means a notification published in the Official Gazette;

(f) "Prescribed" means prescribed by rules made under this Act:

(g) "State Commission" means a State Commission for Protection of Child Rights constituted under section 17.

Chapter II

The National Commission for Protection of Child Rights

3. 1. The Central Government shall, by notification, constitute a body to be known as the National Commission for Protection of Child Rights to exercise the powers conferred on, and to perform the functions assigned to it, under this Act:

2. The Commission shall consist of the following Members, namely :—

(a) a Chairperson who is a person of eminence and has done outstanding work for promoting the welfare of children; and

(b) six Members, out of which at least two shall be women, from the following fields, to be appointed by the Central Government from amongst persons of eminence, ability, integrity, standing and experience in, —

(i) education;

(ii) child health, care, welfare or child development

(iii) juvenile justice or care of neglected or marginalised children or children , with disabilities;

(iv) elimination of child labour or children in distress;

(v) child psychology or sociology; and

(vi) laws relating to children.

(3) The office of the Commission shall be at Delhi.

4. The Central Government shall, by notification, appoint the Chairperson and other Members;

Provided that the Chairperson shall be appointed on the recommendation of a three member Selection Committee constituted by the Central Government under the Chairmanship of the Minister in-charge of the Ministry of Human Resource Development.

5. (1) The Chairperson and every Member shall hold office as such for a term of three years from the date on which he assumes office;

Provided that no Chairperson or a Member shall hold the office for more than two terms:

Provided further that no Chairperson or any other Member shall hold office as such after he has attained—

(a) in the case of the Chairperson, the age of sixty-five years; and (6) in the case of a Member, the age of sixty years.

(2) The Chairperson or a Member may, by writing under his hand addressed to the Central Government, resign his office at any time.

6. The salary and allowances payable to, and other terms and conditions of service of, the Chairperson and Members, shall be such as may be prescribed by the Central Government:

Provided that neither the salary and allowances nor the other terms and conditions of service of the Chairperson or a Member, as the case may be, shall be varied to his disadvantage after his appointment.

7. (1) Subject to the provisions of sub-section (2), the Chairperson may be removed from his office by an order of the Central Government on the ground of proved misbehaviour or incapacity.

(2) Notwithstanding anything contained in sub-section (/), the Central Government may by order remove from office the Chairperson or any other Member, if the Chairperson or, as the case may be. such other Member, —

(a) is adjudged an insolvent; or

(b) engages during his term of office in any paid employment outside the duties of his office; or

(c) refuses to act or becomes incapable of acting; or

(d) is of unsound mind and stands so declared by a competent court; or

(e) has so abused his office as to render his continuance in office detrimental to the public interest; or

(f) is convicted and sentenced to imprisonment for an offence which in the opinion of the Central Government involves moral turpitude; or

(g) is, without obtaining leave of absence from the Commission, absent from three consecutive meetings of the Commission,

(3) No person shall be removed under this section until that person has been given an opportunity of being heard. in the matter.

8. (1) If the Chairperson or, as the case may be, a Member. —

(a) becomes subject to any of the disqualifications mentioned in section 7: or

(b) tenders his resignation under sub-section (2) of section 5, his seat shall thereupon become vacant.

(2) If a casual vacancy occurs in the office of the Chairperson or a Member, whether by-reason of his death, resignation or otherwise, such vacancy shall be filled within a period of ninety days by making afresh appointment in accordance with the provisions of section 4 and the person so appointed shall hold office for the remainder of the term of office for which the Chairperson, or a Member, as the case may be, in whose place he is so appointed would have held that office.

9. No act or proceeding of the Commission shall be invalid merely by reason of—

(a) any vacancy in, or any detect in the constitution of, the Commission; or

(b) any defect in the appointment of a person as the Chairperson or a Member; or

(c) any irregularity in the procedure of the Commission not affecting the merits of the case.

10. (1) The Commission shall meet regularly at its office at such time as the Chairperson thinks fit, but three months shall not intervene between its last and the next meeting.

(2) All decisions at a meeting shall be taken by majority:

Provided that in the case of equality of votes, the Chairperson, or in his absence the person presiding, shall have and exercise a second or casting vote.

(3) If for any reason, the Chairperson, is unable to attend the meeting of the Commission, any Member chosen by the Members present from amongst themselves at the meeting, shall preside.

(4) The Commission shall observe such rules of procedure in the transaction of its business at a meeting, including the quorum at such meeting, as may be prescribed by the Central Government.

(5) All orders and decisions of the Commission shall be authenticated by the Member-Secretary or any other officer of the Commission duly authorised by Member-Secretary in this behalf.

11. (1) The Central Government shall, by notification, appoint an officer not below the rank of the Joint Secretary or the Additional Secretary to the Government of India as a Member-Secretary of the Commission and shall make available to the Commission such other officers and employees as may be necessary for the efficient performance of its functions.

(2) The Member-Secretary shall be responsible for the proper administration of the affairs of the Commission and its day-to-day management and shall exercise and discharge such other powers and perform such other duties as may be prescribed by the Central Government.

(3) The salary and allowances payable to, and the other terms and conditions of service of the Member-Secretary, other officers and employees, appointed for the purpose of the Commission shall be such as may be prescribed by the Central Government.

12. The salaries and allowances payable to the Chairperson and Members and the administrative expenses, including salaries, allowances and pensions payable to the Member-Secretary, other officers and employees referred to in section 11, shall be paid out of the grants referred to in sub-section (1) of section 27.

Chapter III

Functions and Powers of the Commission

13. (1) Commission shall perform all or any of the following functions, namely:

(a) examine and review the safeguards provided by or under any law for the time being in force for the protection of child rights and recommend measures for their effective implementation;

(b) present to the Central Government, annually and at such other intervals, as the Commission may deem fit, reports upon the working of those safeguards;

(c) inquire into violation of child rights and recommend initiation of proceedings in such cases;

(d) examine all factors that inhibit the enjoyment of rights of children affected by terrorism, communal violence, riots, natural disaster, domestic violence, HIV/AIDS, trafficking, maltreatment, torture and exploitation, pornography and prostitution and recommend appropriate remedial measures;

(e) look into the matters relating to children in need of special care and protection including children in distress, marginalised and disadvantaged children, children in conflict with law, juveniles, children without family and children of prisoners and recommend appropriate remedial measures;

(f) study treaties and other international instruments and undertake periodical review of existing policies, programmes and other activities on child rights and make recommendations for their effective implementation in the best interest of children;

(g) undertake and promote research in the field of child rights;

(h) spread child rights literacy among various sections of the society and promote awareness of the safeguards available for protection of these rights through publications, the media, seminars and other available means;

(i) inspect or cause to be inspected any juvenile custodial home, or any other place of residence or institution meant for children, under the control of the Central Government or any State Government or any other authority, including any institution run by a social organisation; where children are detained or lodged for the purpose of treatment, reformation or protection and take up with these authorities for remedial action, if found necessary;

(j) inquire into complaints and take *suo motu* notice of matters relating to.—

(i) deprivation and violation of child rights;

(ii) non-implementation of laws providing for protection and development of children;

(iii) non-compliance of policy decisions, guidelines or instructions aimed at mitigating hardships to and ensuring welfare of the children and to provide relief to such children, or take up the issues arising out of such matters with appropriate authorities; and

(k) such other functions as it may consider necessary for the promotion of child rights and any other matter incidental to the above functions,

(2) The Commission shall not inquire into any matter which is pending before a State Commission or any other Commission duly constituted under any law for the time being in force.

14. (1) The Commission shall, while inquiring into any matter referred to in clause (j) of sub-section (1) of section 13 have all the powers of a civil court trying a suit under the Code of Civil Procedure, 1908 and, in particular, in respect of the following matters, namely:—

(a) summoning and enforcing the attendance of any person and examining him on oath;

(b) discovery and production of any document;

(c) receiving evidence on affidavits;

(d) requisitioning any public record or copy thereof from any court or office; and

(e) issuing commissions for the examination of witnesses or documents.

(2) The Commission shall have the power to forward any case to a Magistrate having jurisdiction to try the same and the Magistrate to whom any such case is forwarded shall proceed to hear the complaint against the accused as if the case has been forwarded to him under section 346 of the Code of Criminal Procedure, 1973.

15. The Commission may take any of the following steps upon the completion of an inquiry held under this Act, namely :—

(i) where the inquiry discloses, the Commission of violation of child rights of a serious nature or contravention of provisions of any law for the time being in force, it may recommend to the concerned Government or authority the initiation of proceedings for prosecution or such other action as the Commission may deem fit against the concerned person or persons;

(ii) approach the Supreme Court or the High Court concerned for such directions, orders or writs as that Court may deem necessary;

(iii) recommend to the concerned Government or authority for the grant of such interim relief to the victim or the members of his family as the Commission may consider necessary.

16. (1) The Commission shall submit an annual report to the Central Government and to the State Government concerned and may at any time submit special reports on any matter which, in it opinion, is of such urgency or importance that it should not be deferred till submission of the annual report.

(2) The Central Government and the State Government concerned, as the case may be, shall cause the annual and special reports of the Commission to be laid before each House of Parliament or the State Legislature respectively, as the case may be, along with a memorandum of action taken or proposed to be taken on the recommendations of the Commission and the reasons for non-acceptance of the recommendations, if any, within a period of one year from the date of receipt of such report..

(3) The annual report shall be prepared in such form, manner and contain such details as may be prescribed by the Central Government

Chapter IV

State Commissions for Protection of Child Rights

17. (1) A State Government may constitute a body to be known as the......... (name of the State) Commission for Protection of Child Rights to exercise the powers conferred upon, and to perform the functions assigned to, a State Commission under this Chapter.

(2) The State Commission shall consist of the following Members, namely:-

(a) a Chairperson who is a person of eminence and has done outstanding work for promoting the welfare of children; and

(b) six Members, out of which at least two shall be women, from the following fields, to be appointed by the State Government from amongst persons of eminence, ability, integrity, standing and experience in,—

(i) education;

(ii) child health, care, welfare or child development;

(iii) juvenile justice or care of neglected or marginalised children or children with disabilities;

(iv) elimination of child labour or children in distress;

(v) child psychology or sociology; and

(vi) laws relating to children,

(3) The headquarter of the State Commission shall be at such place as the State Government may, by notification, specify.

18. The State Government shall, by notification, appoint the Chairperson and other Members:

Provided that the Chairperson shall be appointed on the recommendation of a three Member Selection Committee constituted by the State Government under the Chairmanship of the Minister in-charge of the Department dealing with children.

19. (1) The Chairperson and every Member shall hold office as such for a term of three years from the date on which he assumes office:

Provided that no Chairperson or a Member shall hold the office for more than two terms:

Provided further that no Chairperson or any other Member shall hold office as such after he has attained—

(a) in the case of Chairperson, the age of sixty-five years; and

(b) in the case of a Member, the age of sixty years.

(2) The Chairperson or a Member may, by writing under his hand addressed to the State Government, resign his office at any time.

20. The salaries and allowances payable to, and other terms and conditions of service of, the Chairperson and Members shall be such as may be prescribed by the State Government:

Provided that neither the salary and allowances nor the other terms and conditions of service of the Chairperson or a Member, as the case may be, shall be varied to his disadvantage after his appointment.

21. (1) The State Government shall, by notification, appoint an officer not below the rank of the Secretary to the State Government as the Secretary of the State Commission and shall make available to the State Commission such other officers and employees as may be necessary for the efficient performance of its functions.

(2) The Secretary shall be responsible for the proper administration of the affairs of the State Commission and its day-to-day management and shall exercise and discharge such other powers and perform such other duties as may be prescribed by the State Government.

(3) The salary and allowances payable to, other terms and conditions of service of the Secretary, other officers and employees, appointed for the purpose of the State Commission shall be such as may be prescribed by the State Government.

22. The salaries and allowances payable to the Chairperson and Members and the administrative expenses, including salaries, allowances and pensions payable to the Secretary, other officers and employees referred to in section 21, shall be paid out of the grants referred to in sub-section (j) of section 28.

23. (1) The State Commission shall submit an annual report to the State Government and may at any time submit special reports on any matter which, in its opinion, is of such urgency or importance that it should not be deferred till submission of the annual report.

(2) The State Government shall cause all the reports referred to in sub-section (1) to be-laid before each House of State Legislature, where it consists of two Houses, or where such Legislature consists of one House, before that House along with a memorandum explaining the action taken or proposed to be taken-on the recommendations relating to the State and the reasons for the non-acceptance, if any, of any of such recommendations;

(3) The annual report shall be prepared in such form, manner and contain such details as may be prescribed by the State Government.

24. The provisions of sections 7,8,9,10, sub-section (1) of section 1 3 and sections 14 and 15 shall apply to a State Commission and shall have effect, subject to the following modifications, namely:-

(a) references to "Commission" shall be construed as references to "State Commission";

(b) references to "Central Government" shall be construed as references to "State Government"; and

(c) references to "Member-Secretary" shall be construed as references to "Secretary".

Chapter V

Children's Courts

25. For the purpose of providing speedy trial of offences against children or of violation of child rights, the State Government may, with the concurrence of the Chief Justice of the High Court, by notification, specify at least a court in the State or specify, for each district, a Court of Session to be a Children's Court to try the said offences:

Provided that nothing in this section shall apply if—

(a) a Court of Session is already specified as a special court; or

(b) a special court is already constituted, for such offences under any other law for the time being in force.

26. For every Children's Court, the State Government shall, by notification, specify a Public Prosecutor or appoint an advocate who has been in practice as an advocate for not less than seven years, as a Special Public Prosecutor for the purpose of conducting cases in that Court.

Chapter VI

Finance, Accounts and Audit

27. (1) The Central Government shall, after due appropriation made by Parliament by law in this behalf, pay to the Commission by way of grants such sums of money as the Central Government may think fit for being utilised for the purposes of this Act.

(2) The Commission may spend such sums of money as it thinks fit for performing the functions under this Act, and such sums shall be treated as expenditure payable out of the grants referred to in sub-section (1).

28 (1) The State Government shall, after due appropriation made by Legislature by law in this behalf, pay to the State Commission by way of grants such sums of money as the State Government may think fit for being utilised for the purposes of this Act.

(2) The State Commission may spend such sums of money as it thinks fit for performing the functions under Chapter III of this Act, and such sums shall be treated as expenditure payable out of the grants referred to in sub-section (*l*).

29. (1) The Commission shall maintain proper accounts and other relevant records and prepare an annual statement of accounts in such form as may be prescribed by the Central Government in consultation with the Comptroller and Auditor-General of India,

(2) The accounts of the Commission shall be audited by the Comptroller and Auditor-General at such intervals as may be specified by him and any expenditure incurred in connection with such audit shall be payable by the Commission to the Comptroller and Auditor-General.

(3) The Comptroller and Auditor-General and any person appointed by him in connection with the audit of the accounts of the Commission under this Act shall, have the same rights and privileges and the authority in connection with such audit as the Comptroller and Auditor-General generally has in connection with the audit of Government accounts and, in particular, shall have the right to demand the production of books, accounts, connected vouchers and other documents and papers and to inspect any of the offices of the Commission.

(4) The accounts of the Commission as certified by the Comptroller and Auditor-General or any other person appointed by him in this behalf, together with the audit report thereon shall be forwarded annually to the Central Government by the Commission and the Central Government shall cause the audit report to be laid, as soon as may be after it is received, before each House of Parliament.

30. (1) The State Commission shall maintain proper accounts and other relevant records and prepare an annual statement of accounts in such form as may be prescribed by the State Government in consultation with the Comptroller and Auditor-General of India.

(2) The accounts of the State Commission shall be audited by the Comptroller and Auditor-General at such intervals as may be specified by him and any expenditure incurred in connection with such audit shall be payable by the State Commission to the Comptroller arid Auditor-General.

(3) The Comptroller and Auditor-General and any person appointed by him in connection with the audit of the accounts of the State Commission under this Act shall, have the same rights and privileges and the authority in connection with such audit as the Comptroller and Auditor-General generally has in connection with the audit of Government accounts and, in particular, shall have the right to demand the production of books, accounts, connected vouchers and other documents and papers and to inspect any of the offices of the State Commission.

(4) The accounts of the State Commission as certified by the Comptroller and Auditor-General or any other person appointed by him in this behalf, together with the audit report thereon shall be forwarded annually to the State Government by the State Commission and the State Government shall cause the audit report to be laid, as soon as may be after it is received, before the State Legislature.

Chapter VII

Miscellaneous

31. No suit, prosecution or other legal processing shall lie against the Central Government, the State Government, the Commission, the State Commission, or any Member thereof or any person acting under the direction either of the Central Government, State Government, Commission or the State Commission, in respect of anything which is in good faith done or intended to be done in pursuance of this Act or of any rules made thereunder or in respect of the publication by or under the authority of the Central

Government, State Government, Commission, or the State Commission of any report or paper.

32. Every Member of the Commission, State Commission and every officer appointed in the Commission or the State Commission to exercise functions under this Act shall be deemed to be a public servant within the meaning of section 21 of the Indian Penal Code.

33. (1) In the discharge of its functions under this Act, the Commission shall be guided by such directions on questions of policy relating to national purposes, as may be given to it by the Central Government.

(2) If any dispute arises between the Central Government and the Commission as to whether a question is or is not a question of policy relating to national purposes, the decision of the Central Government thereon shall be final.

34. The Commission shall furnish to the Central Government such returns or other information with respect to its activities as the Central Government may, from time to time, require.

35. (1) The Central Government may, by notification, make rules to carry out the provisions of this Act.

(2) In particular, and without prejudice to the generality of the foregoing power, such rules may provide for all or any of the following matters, namely:-

(a) terms and conditions of service of the Chairperson and Members of the Commission and their salaries and allowances under section 6;

(b) the procedure to be followed by the Commission in the transaction of its business at a meeting under sub-section. (4) of section 10,

(c) the powers and duties which may be exercised and performed by the Member-Secretary of the Commission under sub-section (2) of section 11;

(d) the salary and allowances and other terms and conditions of service of officers and other employees of the Commission under sub-section (3) of section 11; and

(e) form of the statement of accounts and other records to be prepared by the Commission under sub-section (1) of section 29.

(3) Every rule made under this Act shall be laid, as soon as may be after it is made, before each House of Parliament, while it is in session for a total period of thirty days which may be comprised in one session or in two or more successive sessions, and if, before the expiry of the session immediately following the session or the successive sessions aforesaid, both Houses agree in making any modification in the rule or both Houses agree that the rule should not be made, the rule shall thereafter have effect only in such modified form or be of no effect, as the case may be; so, however, that any such modification or annulment shall be without prejudice to the validity of anything previously done under that rule.

36. (1) The State Government may, by notification, make rules to carry out the provisions of this Act.

(2) In particular, and without prejudice to the generality of the foregoing power, such rules may provide for all or any of the following matters, namely:—

(a) terms and conditions of service of the Chairperson and Members of the State Commission and their salaries and allowances under section 20;

(b) the procedure to be followed by the State Commission in the transaction of its business at a meeting under sub-section (4) of section 10 read with section 24;

(c) the powers and duties which may be exercised and performed by the Secretary of the State Commission under sub-section (2) of section. 21;

(d) the salary and allowances and other terms and conditions of service of officers and other employees of the State Commission under sub-section (3) of section 21; and

(e) form of the statement of accounts and other records to be prepared by the State Commission under sub-section (1) of section 30,

(3) Every rule made by the State Government under this section shall be laid, as soon as may be after it is made, before each House of the State Legislature where it consists of two Houses, or where such State Legislature consists of one House, before that House.

37. (1) If any difficulty arises in giving effect to the provisions of this Act, the Central Government may, by order published in the Official Gazette, make such provisions, not inconsistent with the provisions of this Act, as may appear to be necessary for removing the difficulty:

Provided that no order shall be made under this section after the expiry of the period of two years from the date of commencement of this Act.

(2) Every order made under this section shall be laid, as soon as may be after it is made, before each House of Parliament.

Index